EDWARD YOUNG

CASTLE BOOKS

INTRODUCTION

Chess is a very easy game to learn, and it offers perhaps more enjoyment than any other game or sport. In this book you will find all you need to know to play, to enjoy the game, and to hold your own against other friends who play chess.

After reading this book you may feel like going on to more advanced books and improving your skill. However, that is by no means essential. There are many kinds of chess players and many degrees of skill; and it may well be that the average player who sticks to his own immediate circle of friendly opponents, seeking only relaxation and pleasant pastime, may get more fun out of chess than the experts who reach the highest rungs of the chess ladder.

CONTENTS

PART I

THE ELEMENTS OF CHESS

PART II

THE OPENINGS

PART III

HOW TO WIN QUICKLY IN THE OPENINGS

7. OPENING TRAPS

PART IV

THE MIDDLE GAME

PART V

THE ENDGAME

PART I

The Elements of Chess

1. THE BASIC RULES OF CHESS

Chess, the world's most popular game, was invented in India about A.D. 600. From there it spread rapidly into Persia and other Asiatic countries. The Arabs who built a great civilization during the Middle Ages were very fond of chess. They introduced the game wherever they extended their conquests, and thus chess reached Spain, Italy, France and the rest of Europe.

In the nineteenth century the popularity of chess took a powerful upswing with the introduction of master tournaments and matches. The World Championship of chess is now determined by a highly detailed system of world-wide interzonal tournaments, and the devotees of the game are numbered in the many millions.

Although chess has been played for many centuries, it is only since 1800 or so that the rules have become rigorously standardized. We shall now proceed to learn these rules.

The Chessboard and Pieces

Chess is played by two players who move in turn. They play on a chessboard which has 64 squares. All the squares are used in the play. They are coloured alternately, some light ("white"), some dark ("black").

Each player has 16 chessmen. One player ("White") has light-coloured pieces. His opponent ("Black") has dark-coloured pieces.

Each player sets out the pieces along the two horizontal rows of squares nearest to him. Here is the set-up:

DIAGRAM 1
The opening position

Memorize: (1) White always moves first.
(2) The corner square at White's right is always a white square.
Each player has a King, a Queen, two Rooks, two Knights,

13

two Bishops, and eight Pawns. Now, let's see what these pieces do, and how they do it.

The King

Each of the chess pieces moves (and captures) in its own special way.

The King, for example, moves one square in any direction. In Diagram 2 the King can move to any square marked with a cross.

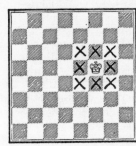

DIAGRAM 2
How the King moves

Now how does the King capture? He captures in the same way he moves.

In Diagram 3 the King has a choice of capturing either Black piece, and displacing that piece on the square where the capture is made.

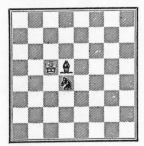

DIAGRAM 3
How the King captures

There are certain limitations on the moves of the King, which is, by the way, the most important of all the chess pieces. In Chapter 2 you will see why this is so.

Now go back to Diagram 1 and see how the White and Black Kings are placed at the beginning of the game. They are in the centre of the back row, and face each other across the board.

The Queen

The crosses in Diagram 4 show how the *Queen* moves.

The Queen moves like the King—but what a difference! Where the King can move one square in any direction, the Queen can move to any square in any direction.

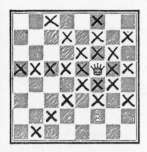

DIAGRAM 4
How the Queen moves

The only limitation on the Queen's move is the presence of a friendly or hostile piece on the line of the Queen's movement. The Queen has to stop on any line if a friendly piece is in the way. The Queen can capture any piece that is on one of the vertical, horizontal, or diagonal lines of its range.

Caution: When we say the Queen can move in any direction, we must add that she must choose one specific direction at each move. This limitation applies to all the chess pieces.

If the Queen moves vertically "up the page" in Diagram 4, she can move right to the edge of the board. But if she moves vertically "down the page," the White Pawn stops her from moving more than two squares.

In Diagram 5 we see how the Queen's enormous range gives her formidable capturing powers.

DIAGRAM 5
How the Queen captures

By moving vertically, the Queen can capture either Black Bishop. By moving on a diagonal, the Queen can capture either Black Knight. By moving horizontally, the Queen can capture either Black Rook.

In the opening position of Diagram 1, each Queen is placed
in the centre of the back row, next to her King. *Memorize* the
rule of " Queen on colour." The White Queen goes on a white
square, the Black Queen goes on a black square.

Again, remember that the Queen can capture only one of these
pieces in a single move. The capture, as we indicated, displaces
the captured piece from its square. This square is then occupied
by the capturing piece.

And again, remember this point about the Queen and the other
chess pieces: they have a choice of moving in many directions,
but they can move in only one direction at a time.

The Rook

Now we come to the *Rook*. The Rook moves vertically (up
and down) or horizontally (left or right). This is shown by the
crosses in Diagram 6.

DIAGRAM 6

How the Rook moves

The Rook captures the same way it moves.

In Diagram 7, the Rook can capture Black's Bishop or Knight.
(The Rook captures only by displacement.)

DIAGRAM 7

How the Rook captures

Going back to the opening position in Diagram 1, you will
note that the Rooks go in the corner of the board when the
pieces are set up to start a game.

The Bishop

The *Bishop* moves diagonally—that is, on squares of the same colour. Remember, the Biship cannot zig-zag—he moves in only one direction at a time. The crosses on Diagram 8 show how the Bishop moves.

DIAGRAM 8
How the Bishop moves

Note that a Bishop is forever limited to squares of the same colour. But turn back to Diagram 1, and you will observe that at the beginning of the game you have two Bishops. One of them moves on white squares, the other moves on black squares.

In Diagram 9 you can see how the Bishop captures.

DIAGRAM 9
How the Bishop captures

The Bishop on the black squares can capture the Queen. The Bishop on the white squares can capture the Γook. (The Bishop captures by displacement).

To repeat: a Bishop on the white squares can move only on white squares and capture only on white squares. A Bishop on the black squares can move only on black squares and capture only on black squares.

At the beginning of the game (Diagram 1), one Bishop is placed next to the King. The other Bishop is placed next to the Queen.

The Knight

The *Knight* is the great exception to the way all the other chess pieces move.

The Knight's move is *always* of the same length—it moves three squares. In Diagram 10, the crosses indicate eight possible Knight moves.

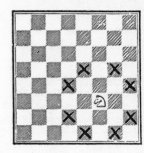

DIAGRAM 10
How the Knight moves

Another peculiarity of the Knight's move is that it moves in two directions at any one move.

You can check the following description of the Knight's move from the location of the crosses on Diagram 10.

The Knight moves two squares up or down and then one square left or right; or two squares left or right and then one square up or down.

Note this: if the Knight is on a white square, he will move to a black square. If he is on a black square, he will move to a white square.

The Knight captures the same way as he moves—on the end-square of his move. Thus, in Diagram 11, he can capture any of the Black Pawns.

DIAGRAM 11
How the Knight captures

The Knight can jump over friendly or hostile pieces located

on the intervening squares of his move. This is another point about this piece that makes it " different."

Of course, when the Knight jumps over a hostile piece, he cannot capture that piece. Only the hostile pieces on the end-square of his move are vulnerable to his attack. Remember this, too: if that end-square is occupied by a friendly piece, the Knight cannot move to that square.

At the beginning of the game (Diagram 1) the Knights are placed between the Rooks and the Bishops.

The Pawn

The *Pawn* is another chessman that involves some interesting exceptions to the general rules.

The Pawn moves in only one direction: *forward*. The White Pawns move towards the Black side; they move " up the page," in our diagrams. The Black Pawns move towards the White side; they move " down the page," in our diagrams.

At the beginning of the game, all the White Pawns are placed in the second horizontal row on White's side (Diagram 1). All the Black Pawns are placed in the second horizontal row on Black's side (Diagram 1).

Whenever a Pawn moves ahead from this second row, it has the *choice* of playing one square or two. Thereafter, it can move only one square ahead.

In Diagram 12 we have three White Pawns and three Black Pawns. Let us see the results of their moves (Diagram 13).

DIAGRAM 12
How the Pawn moves
(*before moving*)

The White Pawn at the extreme right remained unmoved.

The White Pawn in the centre took the option of advancing *one* square at its first move.

The White Pawn at the extreme left took the option of advancing *two squares* at its first move.

DIAGRAM 13
How the Pawn moves
(*after moving*)

Now let us see what the Black Pawns accomplished:

The Black Pawn at the extreme right remained on its original square on the second row.

The Black Pawn in the centre took the option of advancing *two squares* at its first move.

The Black Pawn at the extreme left took the option of advancing *one square* at its first move.

Unlike all the other chessmen, the Pawn does not capture the same way as it moves.

The Pawn's move, as you have seen, is straight ahead. *But the pawn captures one square forward to the right or left.*

Thus, at the extreme right of Diagram 14, White's Pawn can capture Black's Rook.

(Pawns like all the other chess pieces, capture by displacing the captured piece from its square).

DIAGRAM 14
How the Pawn captures
(*before capturing*)

At the extreme left of Diagram 14, neither Pawn can capture the other.

In the centre of Diagram 14, Black's Pawn can capture White's Queen.

Diagram 15 shows the position resulting from the Pawn captures.

DIAGRAM 15
How the Pawn captures
(after capturing)

In this first chapter we have seen how the various chessmen move and capture. In the next chapter we shall see how to win a game of chess.

2. WINNING METHODS IN CHESS

When a King is attacked and cannot escape from attack, he is checkmated. This signifies the loss of the game.

You can therefore see that safeguarding the King is a chess player's most important job.

Check

Whenever a King is attacked, he is said to be in check. In Diagram 16, for example, Black's Queen is giving check to the White King.

DIAGRAM 16
White's King is in check

Whenever your King is in check, you must immediately take measures to get him out of check. One way to get the King out of check is to move him out of the range of the attacking piece. That is what has happened in the position of Diagram 17.

DIAGRAM 17
White's King has moved out of check

But moving the King is by no means the only way to get out of check. You can get out of check by interposing one of your pieces to block the attack on your King.

DIAGRAM 18
White's King has been shielded from check

Still another way to get out of check is to capture the piece that is giving check. The disappearance of the checking piece puts an end to the attack on the King. This is shown in Diagram 19, where White's Bishop has captured Black's Queen and thus put an end to the check.

DIAGRAM 19
White has stopped the check by capturing Black's Queen

Discovered Check

There are special kinds of checks that you need to know about. One of them is called the *discovered check*. (The word " discovered " is used here in the sense of " uncovered ").

As a rule a check results when a piece moves into a position to give check. But the discovered check, shown in Diagram 20, operates on a different principle.

DIAGRAM 20
(White to move)
By advancing his Pawn, White enables his Queen to give check

In the position of Diagram 20, White's Pawn masks the attack of his Queen on the Black King. By advancing, the Pawn opens up the Queen's attack—opens up a discovered check.

What makes the discovered check so dangerous (to the defender) is the possibility of a double attack. When a piece moves to uncover a discovered check, it may be attacking some other undefended unit.

In such cases there is no time to defend. *The check must be taken care of first.* (Since checkmate means the loss of the game, you MUST get out of check if at all possible).

Double Check

Nasty as the discovered check is, it is even nastier if it comes in the form of a *double check*.

Go back for a moment to the position of Diagram 20. Replace the White Pawn with a White Rook. Now have the Rook move to the position it occupies in Diagram 21.

DIAGRAM 21
White gives double check

What happened? The Rook, by moving, has created a discovered check by the Queen. But there is more to it than that. *The Rook is itself giving check!* Thus Black is subjected to double check. His King is checked by the Queen AND the Rook.

To double check there is only one defence. Interposing a piece won't do, because it is impossible to close both lines of attack. Capturing a checking piece won't do, because the other attacker will still be giving check!

The only solution, then, is to move the King to a spot where he is no longer subject to attack. Sometimes it is possible to get the King to a safe hideaway. Sometimes it isn't—and then the game is lost!

Forking Checks

Still another nasty kind of check is the *forking check*, whereby a Knight attacks the King and another piece at the same time.

DIAGRAM 22
A forking check

This type of check illustrates one of the Knight's most formidable powers. Many a game has been lost when two important pieces were caught on the prongs of a Knight's forking check.

Checkmate

We have seen that checkmate means victory for the player who checkmates his opponent's King. So far, however, we have seen checks but no checkmate:

Here is how the Queen forces checkmate:

DIAGRAM 23
Checkmate with the Queen

Why is the position of Diagram 23 a checkmate position?

First, White's Queen is checking (attacking) Black's King. The Queen cannot be captured. No piece can be interposed to block the force of the attack.

What remains for Black? Can his King flee from the attack? No! Wherever the King tries to move, he goes to squares that are in the capturing range of Black's Queen and/or King. A King can never voluntarily expose himself to capture. Hence Black's King cannot move to these squares controlled by the enemy.

So, to sum up: Black's King is in check and has no squares to go to where he will be out of check.

This is checkmate.

The game is over.
Black has lost.

(*Note* that in a game of chess the King is never actually captured. As long as he is in check and cannot escape his fate, that ends the game right then and there.)

In order to bring about this checkmate with the Queen, she needs the active co-operation of her own King. Unless the King is nearby, protecting the Queen (as in Diagram 23), the weaker side's King could get off scot-free by capturing the checking Queen.

How does the Rook force checkmate? Go back to Diagram 23, and substitute a White Rook for the White Queen. Is Black still checkmated? No, for now the Black King can move to the left or right, which takes him out of the Rook's jurisdiction. (Remember that the Rook moves and captures only vertically or horizontally, but not diagonally!)

In Diagram 24 we have a foolproof mating position with the Rook. Let's see why.

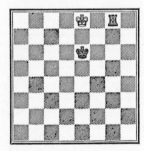

DIAGRAM 24
Checkmate with the Rook

The White King is in check—checked by the Black Rook. White cannot capture the Rook, nor can he interpose a piece to block the line of attack.

Nor can the White King move out of check. If the White King moves along the last row, he is still in check from the Rook. And the White King cannot move to the second row, for the three possible squares available to the White King are all controlled by Black's King.

So again we have a case of checkmate. This time White is on the receiving end of the checkmate, and Black has won the game.

In all these basic checkmates, the weaker side's King must be forced to one of the side rows. In the case of checkmate with the Queen or Rook, it does not matter which square the King is forced to.

However, to checkmate with two Bishops it is not enough to force the King to the edge of the board. *The King must be driven to a corner square.*

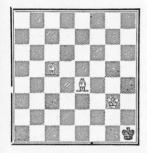

DIAGRAM 25
Checkmate with the two Bishops

Here again we have a perfect checkmating position. Black's King is in check, and there is no way to get him out of check. All the squares within the Black King's range are controlled by the White King and/or the White Bishops. White has checkmated the Black King and thus wins the game.

Another type of basic checkmate—with a Bishop and Knight —also requires cornering the weaker side's King. Diagram 26 shows how such a checkmate works.

DIAGRAM 26
Checkmate with Bishop and Knight

Black's King is in check, and there is no way to get him out of check. All the squares within the Black King's range are controlled by the White King and/or the other two White pieces. Again White has checkmated the Black King and thus wins the game.

From these last examples you have seen that a Queen, aided by her King, can enforce checkmate. This is also true of a single Rook; of both Bishops; and of a Bishop and Knight.

To know this is not enough. For there are pieces which cannot effect checkmate, and this is vitally important information.

A single Bishop, for example, cannot enforce checkmate. Since the Bishop travels on only one colour, the hostile King is safe whenever he occupies a square of the other colour!

A single Knight likewise cannot enforce checkmate. In any given situation there are plenty of squares not controlled by the Knight.

In addition, even BOTH Knights cannot enforce checkmate.

Comparative Values of the Pieces

Now it is time to draw a very important conclusion: the Queen or the Rook can enforce checkmate. The Bishop or Knight cannot. Therefore the Queen or Rook must be stronger than the Bishop or Knight.

Consequently we need some yardstick to show us what pieces are the strongest, and which are less strong. This yardstick will enable us to judge the *comparative* strength of two different pieces.

The following table of comparative values is based on centuries of chess playing and is thoroughly reliable. In this table we give each of the chessmen a standard value. The King is not included in this table, for his value is absolute.

Here are the values:

QUEEN	..	..	..	..	9 points
ROOK ..	..	..	..	..	5 points
BISHOP	..	..	..	..	3 points
KNIGHT	..	..	..	..	3 points
PAWN ..	..	..	..	..	1 point

You can draw many useful conclusions from this table. The main point is that the Queen is by far the most valuable piece. If you lose your Queen by an oversight, you are almost 100 per cent. certain to lose the game—unless your opponent makes an even worse oversight!

The table tells us a great deal about making exchanges. An exchange takes place when you capture one of your opponent's forces, and he captures one of yours in return.

If you are not familiar with the table of values, then exchanges will give you a great deal of trouble. Of course, if you capture a Pawn in return for a Pawn, or a Bishop in return for a Bishop, that exchange is perfectly even. But suppose you capture a Knight, and your opponent captures one of your Bishops! Who gains by such an exchange?

Look at the table. A Bishop is worth 3 points, and so is a

Knight. So the exchange of Bishop for Knight is perfectly even, and neither player loses by it.

On the other hand, suppose you capture a Rook (which is worth 5 points) and your opponent gets only a Pawn (which is worth 1 point) in return. Obviously this is no even exchange, and you have gained considerably by the transaction.

Memorize this simple table of values. By being thoroughly familiar with it, you will always know whether you are ahead or behind in material. This is important; for, *if a player's superiority in material is great enough, he will be able to force checkmate.* Sometimes, when a player has lost too much material, he does not wait for checkmate. Conceding defeat, he " resigns."

Just what amount of superiority in material makes it hopeless to play on?

Given the enormous value of the Queen and her checkmating powers, you may be sure that a player who has lost his Queen without any compensation is sure to lose the game.

Similarly, a player who loses a Rook without exchange is certain to lose the game. And a Bishop or Knight ahead will generally lead to victory.

The Pawn's Promotion Power

But how about a Pawn? Is a player likely to win if he is " only " a Pawn ahead? Remember, the Pawn is the weakest unit on the board. Here we come to one of the most fascinating paradoxes in chess: although the Pawn is the weakest unit on the chessboard, it is potentially the strongest!

This is why: if a Pawn advances progressively from the second row all the way to the eighth row during the course of a game, the Pawn is promoted to a new Queen or Rook or Bishop or Knight. The player who advances the Pawn has the option of promoting to whatever piece he pleases. Naturally he will choose a new Queen, that being the strongest piece on the board. (There are in very rare cases special reasons for promoting to a weaker piece.) Of course, promoting to a new King is impossible.

Thus it is possible to have more than one Queen at the same time. Of course, the chances that a Pawn will remain unscathed throughout the game are not very great. Nevertheless, you have eight Pawns to start with, and if only one of them is preserved from capture, that may well be the Pawn that wins the game. The possibility of changing the humble Pawn into the mighty Queen is one of the factors that makes chess a wonderful fighting game.

In view of this fact, it is very important for you to be familiar with several facets of Pawn promotion. First of all, let's see how it works:

In the position of Diagram 27, White is "only" a Pawn ahead. It is his move, and he advances the Pawn to the last row. It is exchanged for a Queen, and the new Queen gives check. In fact, Black is checkmated! This gives you a graphic idea of the enormous power that is inherent in Pawn protection.

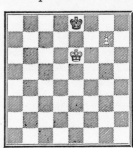

DIAGRAM 27
(*White to move*)
How the Pawn queens

In Diagram 28, we have another impressive example of the Pawn's power.

DIAGRAM 28
(*White to move*)
The power of the Pawn

As you study the position of Diagram 28, imagine that the White Pawn is off the board. In that event White cannot win the game, as his Bishop cannot force checkmate.

But with the Pawn on the board, White wins! He will advance his Pawn to the eighth row, obtaining a new Queen. Black's King cannot capture this Queen, as it is protected by White's Bishop. With the aid of this new Queen, White will force checkmate in short order. Thus the presence of the Pawn makes all the difference in the world.

You can't always be sure of keeping the newly promoted Pawn that has become a Queen. Nevertheless, there is still an advantage to be gained from the new Queen.

The point is neatly made in the play from Diagram 29. Black advances his Queen Pawn to the eighth rank and promotes it to a Queen. White naturally captures the Queen with his Knight. Black then captures White's Knight with his own Knight.

DIAGRAM 29
(*Black to move*)
Pawn promotion wins material

Black's new Queen is no longer on the board, and yet Black has a very easy win. As in Diagram 28, he will advance his remaining Pawn to the last row. The Pawn will be quite safe, escorted by the Black Knight and King.

Thus Black wins easily in Diagram 29, even though his new Queen immediately disappears. In such cases queening is not an end in itself. It is a means of winning material. In this instance Black won White's last remaining piece by queening the passed Pawn.

Familiarity with the queening possibilities outlined here will win many games for you. We turn now to several other important rules of chess.

3. OTHER IMPORTANT RULES

You have learned that the outcome of the game depends on the fate of your King.

It is therefore vital for you to keep the King in as safe a position as possible. For this purpose a special move was invented; it is known as *castling*, and allows you to place your King on a square where it is not easy for the enemy to get at him.

Castling

There are two kinds of castling. The King can castle with the King Rook, or with the Queen Rook.

The King Rook is the Rook nearest to the King in Diagram 1. The Queen Rook is the Rook nearest to the Queen in Diagram 1.

Now let's look at Diagram 30, which shows the position before King-side castling.

DIAGRAM 30
Before castling King-side

(In the following diagrams only White's castling is illustrated. Actually the mechanics of Black's castling is precisely the same).

DIAGRAM 31
After castling King-side

To castle King-side, White moves his King two squares to the right. Then he places the King Rook to the immediate left of his King.

Now let's look at castling from Black's point of view. Since he's at the opposite side of the board, he castles on the King-side by moving his King two squares to the left, and placing the King Rook at the immediate right of his King.

Once both players have castled on the King-side, their Kings face each other across the length of the same vertical row (called a " file ").

Castling on the Queen-side presents much the same kind of picture.

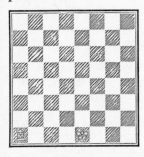

DIAGRAM 32
Before castling Queen-side

To castle on the Queen-side, White moves his King two squares to the left, and then places his Queen Rook to the immediate right of his King. This leads to the position of Diagram 33.

DIAGRAM 33
After castling Queen-side

When Black castles on the Queen-side, he moves his King two squares to the right, and then places his Queen Rook to the immediate left of his King.

After both Kings castle on the Queen-side, they face each other across the board along the same file.

As a general rule, you will be castling on the King-side. In most games this is safer than castling on the Queen-side.

A valuable point to remember is that since castling assures the safety of your King, you do well to castle at the earliest opportunity.

Castling is an important and desirable move, but it is hedged about with certain limitations. Sometimes castling is impossible for the time being. Sometimes it is altogether impossible.

First let's consider the situations where castling is temporarily impossible.

You cannot castle in reply to a check. However, you may be able to castle later on when your King is out of check.

You cannot castle when the King's move would place him on a square controlled by an enemy piece. However, you may be able to castle later on when that square is no longer under enemy control.

You cannot castle if your King is to pass over a square controlled by the enemy. Again, you may be able to castle at a later stage when that square is no longer controlled by one of your opponent's pieces.

Now, before we examine the last exception, take another look at Diagrams 30 and 32. You will note that in these "before-castling" positions *the squares between the King and the Rook are empty.*

You cannot castle whenever any of the squares between the King and Rook are occupied. It does not matter whether the piece occupying either intervening square is your own or your opponent's. The prohibition applies in either event.

However, if at some later point the squares between the King and the Rook are emptied, you may then be able to castle.

All these exceptions are temporary. But there are two cases when castling is permanently ruled out.

If your King has already moved, then you can never castle for the rest of the game.

If your King has not moved but one of the Rooks has, then you cannot castle with *that* Rook. However, if the other Rook hasn't moved, you may be able to castle with that Rook.

The main point to keep in mind, then, is to avoid moving your King. For if you do that you forfeit your right to castle.

Capturing in Passing

Now let's turn to another special kind of move. This one involves the Pawn.

You recall from Diagram 14 that the Pawn captures ahead one square to the left or right.

In addition to this orthodox method of capture, the Pawn can capture *en passant* (" in passing ") in certain situations.

To illustrate a capture in passing, we're going to show how it's done by a White Pawn: but you will bear in mind that Black Pawns can also capture in passing.

Before we study this method, remember that *only a Pawn can capture in passing*; and that *it can only capture a Pawn in passing*.

The position of Diagram 34 shows us the basic situation for a capture in passing.

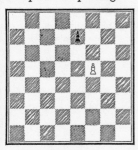

DIAGRAM 34
(*Black to move*)
Basic position for capturing in passing

The Pawn that will ultimately be captured must be on its second "rank," as the horizontal rows are called. This role is played by the Black Pawn in Diagram 34.

The Pawn that is to do the capturing must be on its fifth rank, and on a file that is next to the file of the Pawn to be captured You will note in Diagram 34 that the Pawns are on adjacent files. (The White Pawn is to do the capturing).

Now, suppose that in the position of Diagram 34 Black's Pawn advances one square. In that case, White can capture the Pawn—a plain case of straight capturing as in Diagram 14.

However, to illustrate the principle of capturing in passing, let us imagine that the Black Pawn advances *two squares*.

DIAGRAM 35
(*White to move*)
Black's Pawn has advanced two squares

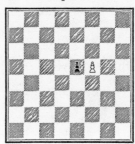

In the position of Diagram 35 White has the option of capturing the Black Pawn as if it had advanced one square instead of two. If he makes the capture, we get the position of Diagram 36.

You see from Diagram 36 that capturing in passing leads to the same position that would have resulted from the Black Pawn's advancing only one square.

DIAGRAM 36
White has captured in passing

Capturing in passing, as has been pointed out, is an option. However, it is an option that must be exercised *at once*. If you turn down your option of capturing in passing, the opportunity is gone for good.

Chess Notation

To know how to record the moves of chess is not part of the rules. You can play chess for a whole lifetime without knowing chess notation.

However, it is impossible to record games and positions without knowing chess notation. In fact, it is impossible to study chess books and improve your play without knowing chess notation. Therefore this seems a good time to learn chess notation.

The principle of chess notation is quite simple: *every square on the chessboard has a name*. Indeed, every square on the board has two names, depending on whether you are looking at it from the White side or the Black side.

These names are derived from the opening position (Diagram 1).

Note the situation of White's forces in the opening position. His pieces are all on the *first* rank; his Pawns are all on the *second* rank.

The name of the King's square is K1.

The Bishop next to the King is known as the King Bishop (KB). The King Bishop's square is KB1.

The Knight next to the King Bishop is the King Knight

(KN). The King Knight's square is KN1. (Thus you see that the abbreviation for Knight is " N ").

The Rook next to the King Knight is the King Rook (KR) and it stands on KR1.

The Queen (Q) stands on Q1.

The Bishop next to the Queen is the Queen Bishop (QB). It stands on QB1.

The Knight next to the Queen Bishop is the Queen Knight (QN). It stands on QN1.

The Rook next to the Queen Knight is the Queen Rook (QR). It stands on QR1.

Remember that the squares always have the same names, regardless of whether the original pieces are on them or not.

The Pawn in front of the King is called the King Pawn. It stands on K2. Here is a table of the names of the Pawns and the names of the squares they occupy at the beginning of the game:

Pawn					Square
Queen Rook Pawn (QRP)..	..	..	..	..	QR2
Queen Knight Pawn (QNP)	..	..	..	..	QN2
Queen Bishop Pawn (QBP)	..	..	..	..	QB2
Queen Pawn (QP)	..	..	..	..	Q2
King Pawn (KP)	..	..	..	..	K2
King Bishop Pawn (KBP)	..	..	..	..	KB2
King Knight Pawn (KNP)	..	..	..	..	KN2
King Rook Pawn (KRP)	..	..	..	..	KR2

By now you can probably guess at the system used for naming all the squares. The vertical rows on the board are named for the pieces standing on them at the beginning of the game.

Thus, the file in which the King stands is the King file. The squares in this file are K1, K2, K3, K4, K5, K6, K7, K8. The squares on the Queen Rook file are QR1, QR2, QR3, etc., up to QR8.

If the King Pawn advances two squares, we record the move as " P–K4." (We don't have to specify which Pawn, because the King Pawn is the only one that can go to K4).

The ranks, or horizontal rows, are named for numbers. Thus all the squares in the first rank end in 1. All the squares in the second rank end in 2; the squares in the third rank end in 3; the squares in the fourth rank end in 4, etc.

Now, how about Black? He follows the same system. Note, however, that when he moves *he numbers the squares from his side of the board.*

The square that is K4 from White's side of the board is K5 from Black's side of the board. The square that is K5 from White's side of the board is K4 from Black's side of the board. If Black moves his King Pawn two squares, we write that move "... P–K4." (The three dots in front of the move show that it is a Black move).

You will always have the moves clear if you remember that *each player counts off his moves from his side of the board.*

You have already seen that each piece and Pawn has its special abbreviation. There are a number of other abbreviations:

x (captures)   ch (check)
– (moves to)   dis ch (discovered check)
! (a good move)   dbl ch (double check)
? (a bad move)   e.p. (captures in passing)

Just to get the feel of chess notation, let's play over a very short game.

	WHITE	BLACK
1	P–K4	P–K4
2	B–B4	B–B4
3	Q–R5	N–QB3
4	QxBP mate	

Diagram 37 shows the final position.

DIAGRAM 37
(*Final position*)

Check this final position very carefully to make sure that you thoroughly understand how each move was made. (In the final position, Black cannot capture the White Queen because it is guarded by White's Bishop on QB4).

Drawn Games

Not every game of chess ends in victory for either side. You will recall that in our discussion of Diagram 28 it was pointed out that without the White Pawn there could be no checkmate. In other words, the game would bc drawn.

There are several other ways in which a game of chess may end in a draw. Let's go through them briefly.

A game may be drawn by agreement. If both players are satisfied with a draw, they can end the game right then and there. This often happens when both players feel they have no likelihood of winning the game.

A game may be called a draw if a player can show that no capture has been made, and no Pawn moved, in the last 50 moves.

Naturally this rule will be invoked only under extraordinary circumstances, and these need to be explained. Suppose a player has a considerable advantage in material and doesn't know how to win with this material. Without this rule he could drift on to Doomsday. The rule therefore penalizes lack of skill.

To invoke this rule it is necessary to have a written score of the game; otherwise there is no way of knowing when the 50 moves have elapsed.

Another type of draw arises when a position has occurred twice, and is about to occur for the third time with the same player on the move each time. Again, as a practical proposition, it would hardly be possible to claim this kind of draw without having a written record of the game.

The draw by threefold repetition is hardly ever seen in friendly games. It occurs mostly in master tournaments and matches.

The perpetual check is a fairly frequent method of ending a game in a draw. This occurs in positions where one player has the power of checking continually, while his opponent is unable to put an end to the series of checks. Diagram 38 illustrates the mechanics of a perpetual check.

Black has an enormous plus in material, and may therefore reasonably hope to win the game.

Since White is hopelessly behind in material, he is naturally very happy to get a draw by perpetual check. This is how he does it:

He plays 1 Q–K8ch, and Black answers 1 . . . K–R2.

Now White checks again: 2 Q–R5ch, and Black replies 2 . . . K–N1.

This brings us back to the position of Diagram 38!

Now White plays 3 Q–K8ch, and Black answers 3 . . . K–R2.

Once more, after 4 Q–R5ch and the reply 4 . . . K–N1, we are back again to the position of Diagram 38. Obviously this can go on for ever, so to save further time the game is called a draw at this point.

DIAGRAM 38
(*White to move*)
Perpetual check

There is still one other kind of draw; it is known as " stale-mate."

You will recall from Diagram 23 that checkmate occurs when the King is attacked and cannot move to a square safe from enemy attack.

Stalemate positions are slightly different, but the difference is very important. We get a stalemate position when the King is not attacked, but has no safe square to go to. Diagram 39 shows such a position.

DIAGRAM 39
(*Black to move*)
Stalemate

Black's King is not attacked. However, it is Black's turn to move. The King has no safe square to go to. Any square he can move to is attacked by the enemy. This is stalemate: the game is drawn, despite White's overwhelming advantage in material.

(*Note* that if it were White's move, this would not be stale-mate! It is only when the weaker side's King *has* to move and can't that the stalemate rule is applied.)

Stalemate is also in a sense a penalty on a player who lacks the skill to apply his advantage incisively.

4. THE TECHNIQUES FOR WINNING QUICKLY

In this chapter we want to get the feel of chess as it is actually played. In this way we will get a practical grasp of the game. The best method is to study some short, decisive games and see why they came to such an abrupt end. Just what was the mistake that lost the game? Just how did the winner go about punishing the mistake?

GAME 1: RUY LOPEZ

WHITE	BLACK
1 P–K4	. . .

It is always good policy to start by playing out a centre Pawn. This gives you a strong grip on the centre squares, the most important sector of the board.

In addition, playing out a centre Pawn opens up lines for your pieces. In this case, White opens lines for his King Bishop and his Queen.

1 . . .	P–K4

Black imitates White and gets the same worthwhile results from moving out his King Pawn.

2 N–KB3	. . .

Another move to be strongly recommended. White develops a piece, gains time by attacking Black's King Pawn, and achieves still another object.

What is that object? White wants to castle early, so as to create a safe haven for his King. By playing out his King Knight promptly, he begins to clear the space between his King and King Rook, so that he can soon castle.

2 . . .	N–QB3

A good move. Black develops a piece—that alone is enough to make the move a good one.

But Black does more: he defends his attacked King Pawn. For if White plays NxP??, Black replies . . . NxN and White has lost a Knight for a Pawn. This would be a grievous loss of material for White.

3 B–N5	. . .

Another fine developing move. White brings out his Bishop

to an aggressive post. He prepares for castling, getting his King into safety.

3 ...   N–B3

But Black is playing well too. He develops another piece, and meanwhile he attacks White's King Pawn.

Both players have been bringing out their pieces with admirable rapidity.

4 P–Q3   ...

Another good move. White opens up the diagonal for his Queen Bishop, and at the same time he protects his King Pawn from attack.

DIAGRAM 40
(Black to move)
Black plans a trap

If Black tries ... NxP?? he loses his Knight (in return for a mere Pawn) after the reply PxN.

Instead, Black tries a trap.

4 ...   N–K2?

This move is wrong because it moves a piece for the second time and thus slows up the development of Black's pieces.

Black's Knight move is also wrong because it blocks the development of Black's King Bishop.

And Black's trap—where is it? The trap consists in the fact that Black has left his King Pawn undefended.

Now White's problem is: should he capture the completely undefended King Pawn?

White can let this Pawn severely alone and make any number of satisfactory alternative moves. For one thing, he can castle right now and get his King into safety.

White is also aware that he ought to avoid moving the Knight a second time in the opening. But, as so many others have told themselves before, he says to himself, "After all, a Pawn's a Pawn!"

5 NxP??   P–B3!

Black's last move shows what he had in mind. He attacks White's Bishop, and in the event of the Bishop's retreat he will play . . . Q–R4ch, giving check and at the same time attacking White's advanced and precariously situated Knight.

White realises that he has blundered, and therefore he craftily sets a counter-trap.

| 6   N–B4!? | . . . |

A noble try, but it shouldn't work.

| 6   . . . | PxB??? |

Black is too greedy!

| 7   N–Q6 mate |

Black is checkmated. He cannot capture the checking Knight, and his King cannot flee from the check.

DIAGRAM 41
(*Final position*)
The trapper trapped!

Now, return to the position after 6 N–B4!?

Black should play 6 . . . N–N3. This stops White's Knight from checking, as Black's King Bishop is now functioning on its diagonal.

With White's main threat gone, he must save his menaced Bishop.

Hence the retreat 7 B–R4 is indicated. But then comes P–N4 "forking" White's Bishop and Knight. This compels the win of a piece for Black, leaving White with a lost game.

From this eventful seven-move game, you can see that a great deal can happen in chess in a few moves!

GAME 2:   THREE KNIGHTS' GAME

WHITE	BLACK
1 P–K4	P–K4
2 N–KB3	N–QB3

So far the players have followed the course of the previous game. The opening play with the centre Pawn is always excellent policy, as we have seen. The development of the Knights is also to be recommended.

>   3   N–B3   . . .

Here White branches off. But he is developing another piece, so the move is quite satisfactory.

>   3   . . .   B–B4

Black develops his King Bishop—excellent play. *Always be on the alert to bring out your pieces quickly during the opening stage.*

Now White plays a move that looks like a crude blunder.

>   4   NxP!?   . . .

Apparently this loses the Knight for a mere Pawn.

>   4   . . .   NxN

Black captures—why not?

>   5   P–Q4!

Now we see what White had in mind: his Queen Pawn " forks " Black's Knight and Bishop. He therefore wins back his piece!

DIAGRAM 42
(*Black to move*)
White recovers his sacrificed piece

Black should play 5 . . . B–Q3. Then, after 6 PxN and 6 . . . BxP the game would be even.

>   5   . . .   Q–K2?

It is one of the most important rules of opening play that *the Queen should not be played out too early.*

What is the point of the rule?

Experience has shown that when the Queen is played out too early, she is vulnerable to the attacks of the enemy's forces.

That is just what happens here.

>   6   N–Q5!   . . .

Attacking the Black Queen.

If Black replies 6 . . . Q–K3??? White's Knight captures the Black Queen Bishop Pawn with check—a forking check that wins the Black Queen!

	6 . . .	Q–Q3
	7 PxB	. . .

Again the Black Queen is attacked!

| | 7 . . . | QxP |

Black shrugs off the attack. Now that he has regained his lost material, he is content. But his satisfaction is short-lived.

| | 8 B–KB4! | . . . |

White develops his Bishop with gain of time. He attacks Black's exposed Knight.

| | 8 . . . | P–Q3 |

Black defends his attacked Knight—what could be more natural?

And yet Black now finds that his Queen is lost by force!

| | 9 P–QN4! | Q–B3 |

Any other Queen move loses at once. The Queen is still lost, but the proof is rather subtle.

DIAGRAM 43

(*White to move*)

White wins the Black Queen by a combination of a pin and a fork

| | 10 B–QN5!!! | . . . |

Pinning the Queen on the same line with the Black King. This leaves Black no choice. He must capture the pinning Bishop.

	10 . . .	QxB
	11 NxPch	. . .

A forking check, as in Diagram 22. The Knight check attacks Black's King, Queen, and Rook. Black must move his King, whereupon White continues 12 NxQ, with an enormous material advantage.

Rather than play on in such a hopeless situation, Black resigned. His primary fault was playing out his Queen much too early in the game. The result was that his Queen became a target attack for White's pieces.

GAME 3: GIUOCO PIANO

WHITE	BLACK
1 P–K4	P–K4
2 N–KB3	N–QB3

Both sides have started the game on approved lines. Now White varies from the first two games.

3 B–B4	. . .

An excellent development of the Bishop. At this square it aims at Black's King Bishop 2 square, which is the most vulnerable point in Black's game. It often happens, especially in games between inexperienced players, that this square, right next to Black's King, can be stormed by a concentrated attack of White's pieces.

3 . . .	B–B4

Likewise an excellent developing move. Now, both sides are ready to castle and thus get their Kings into safety.

White would like to play N–N5, attacking Black's King Bishop Pawn a second time.

However, to play the Knight to Knight 5 right now would be a silly blunder. Black would merely reply 4 . . . QxN, winning a piece.

4 P–Q3	. . .

White opens up the diagonal for his Queen Bishop. Thus he will be able to develop that piece and he can also guard the Knight if it goes to Knight 5.

DIAGRAM 44

(*Black to move*)

Black plays his King Knight to the wrong square

4   ...   KN–K2?

Although this move has the virtue of developing a piece, it
is a poor move.

The right way to play the Knight, for reasons that will soon
become clear, is 4 . . . N–B3!

5   N–N5   ...

White goes ahead with his plan. He attacks Black's Bishop
Pawn twice, while the Pawn is defended only once.

Black needs an extra defence for his King Bishop Pawn.
The most obvious way to obtain that defence is to castle, enabling
the King Rook to defend the King Bishop Pawn. So Black
castles.

5   ...   Castles

Now that Black has castled, his King Bishop Pawn is attacked
twice and defended twice.

Yet Black is headed for trouble. Had he played 4 . . . N–B3!
it would be impossible for White to strengthen at this point
with 6 Q–R5. (The Knight at King Bishop 3 is one of the most
effective defensive pieces on the board).

DIAGRAM 45

(*White to move*)

**Black's defence fails because he has
played . . . KN-K2 instead of . . . N-B3**

6   Q R5!   ...

Taking full advantage of Black's faulty 4 . . . KN–K2?

White's Queen move attacks Black's King Bishop Pawn a
third time, and also threatens 7 QxRP mate. Now you can fully
appreciate the havoc caused by Black's failure to play his Knight
to King Bishop 3.

6   ...   P–KR3

The only move to stop checkmate.

7   NxP   ...

If now 7 . . . RxN White replies 8 QxRch remaining with
a Rook and Pawn for a Knight—a sizeable advantage in material.

Black tries a different way, and loses even more rapidly

    7 ...   Q K1?

This allows White to win Black's Queen by 8 N–Q6 dis ch.

    8 NxP dbl ch!   ...

White refuses the Queen—he has something even better. That "something" must be checkmate.

    8 ...   K–R2

Remember that the only possible reply to a double check is to move your King.

    9 N–B7 dis ch   K–N1
    10 Q–R8 mate

Why is this checkmate?

The position of Diagram 46 is checkmate because White's Queen is guarded by his advanced Knight, which in turn is guarded by his Bishop at Queen Bishop 4. Black's King is in check and has no escape.

DIAGRAM 46

(*Final position*)

Black has been punished for his faulty Knight move

The important lesson to be learned from this instructive game is that the absence of the valuable protective Knight from the square King Bishop 3 can lead to very serious trouble.

GAME 4: PONZIANI OPENING

    WHITE   BLACK
    1 P–K4   P–K4
    2 N–KB3   N–QB3

Again both players have started the game in recommended fashion, but White's next move is inferior.

    3 P–B3   ...

Not the best. The defect of this move is that the Queen Bishop Pawn now occupies the square that should be reserved for White's Knight.

3 . . .   P–Q4!

Black is not afraid of the reply 4 PxP, which he will answer with 4 . . . QxP.

Ordinarily, as we saw in Game 2, it is poor policy to develop the Queen early in the game. For example, in the position of Diagram 47, if White's Queen Bishop Pawn were still at its original square, White could play 4 PxP, QxP. Then he could punish Black's early Queen move by playing out his Queen Knight and threatening to capture Black's Queen.

DIAGRAM 47
(*White to move*)
Black is playing aggressively

But this is all hypothetical. In the actual position we are dealing with (Diagram 47), White's Queen Bishop Pawn is already at Queen Bishop 3. Hence Black need not be afraid to bring out his Queen early in the game.

4 Q–R4   . . .

It is easy to see from the previous discussion that it is pointless for White to play PxP.

By playing his Queen out to Queen Rook 4, White pins Black's Queen Knight.

4 . . .   PxP
5 NxP   . . .

Taking advantage of the fact that Black's Knight at Queen Bishop 3 is pinned.

Black seems to be in trouble, for his King Pawn is attacked, and in addition his Queen Knight is attacked twice and only defended once.

5 . . .   Q–Q4

Very economically played. The Queen protects the Black King Pawn and the Black Queen Knight, and in addition attacks White's advanced Knight!

6   B–N5   . . .

White's reply is tricky. He reinforces the pin on Black's Queen Knight and *seems* to leave his own advanced Knight in the lurch.

But this is deceptive. For if Black plays 6 . . . QxN White captures the Black Knight with his Bishop, giving check. Black recaptures with his Queen Knight Pawn. Thereupon White plays 8 QxBPch with double attack on the Black King and the Black Queen Rook.

So Black is prudent and gives his Queen Knight additional protection.

6 . . .   KN–K2

Now that his Queen Knight is amply guarded, Black really threatens to play . . . QxN.

7   P–KB4   . . .

Protecting his advanced Knight.

But White does more: he threatens 8 B–B4, driving off Black's Queen and making possible the capture of Black's King Bishop Pawn.

Black's reply to this tricky move is equally tricky.

7 . . .   B–Q2!

The point of this move is that if White guilelessly plays 8 B–B4, Black replies 8 . . . NxN, for now his Queen Knight is no longer pinned.

In that case Black wins a piece. White therefore decides to simplify.

8   NxB   KxN

Now Black, having moved his King, can no longer castle. But this does not trouble him, for he has more pieces out and his position is more promising.

9   Castles   N–B4

With the fearful threat of 10 . . . B–B4ch; 11 K–R1, N–N6ch; 12 PxN, Q–R4 mate.

10   P–QN4   . . .

This is played to stop . . . B–B4ch.   But Black has a devilish plan.

10   . . .   P–QR4!

Black's threat is 11 . . . PxP!!; 12 QxR, B–B4ch with a discovered attack winning White's Queen.

11   K–R1   . . .

White hopes to parry the attack by moving his Queen off the checking diagonal. But Black's plan is deeper.

DIAGRAM 49
(*Black to move*)
Black has a very brilliant winning plan

11   . . .   PxP!!

Giving away a Rook—but he has a reason.

12   QxR   B–B4!!

Another discovered attack, which gives away another Rook.

13   QxR   N–N6 ch!

And still another sacrifice.

14   PxN   Q–R4 mate

Beautiful play. White's Queen is far away on a fishing expedition. White's other pieces are scattered, useless, or still on their home squares.

Black, on the other hand, makes the most of his excellent disposition of his forces. Thus he is able to drive White into an early checkmate.

GAME 5: PHILIDOR'S DEFENCE

WHITE	BLACK
1 P–K4	P–K4
2 N–KB3	...

So far the game has gone along recommended lines. With his next move Black branches off, and not to his advantage.

2 ...   P–Q3

This is inferior to 2 ... N–QB3, which brings out a piece—always a desirable achievement—and at the same time leaves open the diagonal of Black's King Bishop for future development.

After 2 ... P–Q3, however, we have a different kind of situation. It is true that the Pawn move prevents White from capturing the Black King Pawn. But 2 ... P–Q3 has two drawbacks: Black has not developed his Queen Knight, and he has blocked the diagonal of his King Bishop.

DIAGRAM 50

(*White to move*)

Black has seriously hampered the development of his pieces

3 B–B4   ...

Note the difference between this Bishop and Black's King Bishop. White's Bishop has a clear, effective diagonal, pointing menacingly at Black's King Bishop 2 square. Black's King Bishop is hemmed in by the Black Pawn at the Queen 3 square and has no scope to speak of.

3 ...   B–N5

Black at last develops a piece. He pins White's King Knight so as to limit the activity of White's forces.

4 N–B3   ...

As Black has only one piece developed in comparison to White's three, it is important for Black to develop his pieces rapidly. He must catch up with White in development.

A good move for this purpose would be 4 . . . N–KB3. This would serve the primary purpose of speeding up Black's development. It would also help to prepare for Black's castling, by removing one of the obstacles that now stand between Black's King and his King Rook. (See Diagrams 30–31 for a review of castling).

Finally, the Black King Knight, if brought to the King Bishop 3 square, would serve the same valuable function that was emphasized in Game 3.

4 . . .   P–KR3??

Black not only neglects his development and the safety of his King—he actually gives White the opportunity for a brilliant and decisive attack.

5 NxP!!   . . .

DIAGRAM 51

(*Black to move*)
Should Black accept White's Queen sacrifice?

Note that White is not only offering his Queen—whether by oversight or intention!! He is also attacking Black's pinning Bishop.

Thus if Black declines the Queen and instead plays 5 . . . PxN, White replies 6 QxB and he has gained a clear Pawn and remains with a very superior game.

Black decides to capture the Queen.

5 . . .   BxQ
6 BxPch   . . .

The Black King cannot capture this Bishop, which is guarded by White's advanced Knight.

6 . . .   K–K2

The only move, as he cannot play 6 . . . K–Q2 because that square is in the jurisdiction of White's advanced Knight.

7 N–Q5 mate.

DIAGRAM 52
(*Final position*)
Black's King is checkmated!

This is a checkmating position, because every possible move of the Black King is covered by one of the White pieces.

This game shows the importance of developing pieces rapidly and guarding the King from hostile attack.

GAME 6: KING'S GAMBIT

WHITE	BLACK
1 P–K4	P–K4
2 P–KB4	. . .

White's second move comes as something of a surprise. It offers something for nothing. Such opening moves are known as *gambits*, from an Italian word that means " to trip up."

DIAGRAM 53
(*Black to move*)
White offers a gambit

Now there must be a reason for offering something for nothing. What compensation is White getting, or does he hope to get?

White looks forward to the opening of the King Bishop file. After playing his King Bishop to Queen Bishop 4, White will castle, placing his King Rook on the King Bishop file.

If he can capture the Black Pawn which will be in his King Bishop 4 square, White anticipates a powerful attack on the King Bishop file. This attack is to be concentrated on Black's weak point, the King Bishop 2 square. (We have seen from Games 3 and 5 that this point can be vulnerable to a sharp attack.)

Whether the game will proceed as White wants it to, will, of course depend on whether Black plays well or badly.

2 ...	PxP
3 N–KB3	...

Always a good developing move. And, of course, since White hopes to attack on the King Bishop file, he wants to castle as soon as possible.

3 ...	P–KN4

Black does not mean to lose the Pawn he has won. He is going to put up a determined fight to hold on to it, and he even defends it before it is attacked!

4 B–B4	...

The game seems to be building up to the same ominous picture we saw in the previous game. White has two pieces in active play, Black has none. If Black is exposed to attack in the next few moves, he may be unable to offer satisfactory resistance. His pieces on the back rank are like a reserve army that is far, far from the scene of battle.

Black should now play 4 ... B–N2. This would start his development and would be the first step toward castling and getting his King into safety. Instead, he blunders badly.

4 ...	P–KB3?
5 NxP!	...

DIAGRAM 54
(*White to move*)
Black has exposed his King to a deadly attack

White's unexpected sacrifice of the Knight leaves Black without a good defence. He can hardly refuse the Knight, in view of White's threatened 6 N–B7, forking Black's Queen and Rook.

There is an even deadlier threat: 6 Q–R5ch. With unerring

aim White has fastened on Black's vulnerable spot, the King Bishop 2 square. So Black captures the invading Knight.

5	. . .	PxN
6	Q–R5ch	K–K2

The only move. But now Black's King is " taken for a ride " and soon checkmated.

7	Q–B7ch	K–Q3

Again forced. The King always cuts a sorry figure when he is forced out into the open and exposed to the attack of hostile pieces without enjoying any protection by his own forces.

8	Q–Q5ch	K–K2

Again forced.

9	Q–K5 mate

DIAGRAM 55
(*Final position*)
Black is checkmated

Black's King is checkmated, because every possible square he can move to is commanded by White's Queen or Bishop.

White has exploited Black's drastic failure to bring out his pieces and to protect his King.

GAME 7: FALKBEER COUNTER GAMBIT

	WHITE	BLACK
1	P–K4	P–K4
2	P–KB4	. . .

The same opening position as in the previous game.

2	. . .	P–Q4

Instead of accepting the gambit as in Game 6, Black offers a counter gambit.

3	N–KB3	. . .

White does not forget to develop his pieces.

    3 ...   QPxP
    4 NxP   B-Q3

Black likewise concentrates on development.

    5 P-Q4   ...

This gives Black the option of capturing in passing with his King Pawn.

    5 ...   PxP e.p.

Black accepts the option. Diagram 56 shows the resulting position.

DIAGRAM 56

(*White to move*)
Black has just captured White's Queen Pawn in passing with his King Pawn

    6 BxP   N-KB3
    7 Castles   Castles
    8 N-QB3   ...

Thus far both players have concentrated admirably on their development, and have both castled to bring their Kings into safety.

But now Black sees a chance to win a Pawn, and he leaves the straight and narrow path of effective development.

DIAGRAM 57

(*Black to move*)
Black mistakenly indulges in Pawn-grabbing

8	...	BxN
9	PxB	Q–Q5ch?
10	K–R1	QxP .
11	B–KB4	...

Black has won a Pawn, but he has lost valuable time. White has an enormous lead in development, and he now gains further time by attacking Black's Queen. Note that his Rook can strike along the open King Bishop file.

| 11 | ... | Q–QB4 |

Naturally Black removes his Queen from attack.

| 12 | BxBP! | ... |

Now White regains his sacrificed Pawn.

In the position of Diagram 58, White has offered a Bishop—apparently free of charge. Even if Black feels like turning down this gift, he has to guard against a curious threat at White's disposal.

DIAGRAM 58

(*Black to move*)
White threatens B-Q6

In Diagram 58, White is threatening a Bishop fork by 13 B–Q6, attacking the Black Queen and a Black Rook. If Black answers that move with 13 ... QxB, there follows 14 BxPch with a discovered attack on Black's Queen which wins that piece.

Since Black is bothered by this threat, and since he can see no point to White's twelfth move, he captures the annoying Bishop.

| 12 | ... | QxB |
| 13 | RxN! | ... |

And now another sacrifice in material; this time White gives up a Rook for a Knight. The purpose of this sacrifice is to smash up the bulwark of Pawns that guard Black's castled King.

With the position opened up, and with Black's development

sadly in arrears, it will be a hopeless task to defend against White's powerful attack.

	13 ...	PxR
	14 Q–R5	...

Threatens 15 QxRP mate. Black has no good defence.

One way for Black to try to stave off the threat of mate is to play 14 ... R–K1, so that after 15 QxRPch his King can escape by ... K–B1. But then White plays 16 N–Q5 (attacking the Black Queen) and at the same time threatening 17 Q–R8 mate, since Black's King can no longer escape.

Thus 14 ... R–K1 is ruled out as a defence.

Perhaps 14 ... R–Q1 can be tried, with the same idea of making room for the Black King, and also with the idea of preventing White's deadly N–Q5.

DIAGRAM 59

(Black to move)
How should Black defend against the mating threat?

But after 14 ... R–Q1, White plays 15 QxRPch, and after 15 ... K–B1 he plays 16 R–K1. (This prevents the Black King from escaping from the threatened 17 Q–R8 mate.) Then if Black tries to block the King file with 16 ... B–K3, White replies 17 RxB! winning—for if 17 ... PxR; 18 QxQ—with overwhelming material superiority.

	14 ...	P–B4

The only alternative. Black tries as best he can to repair the ravages caused by the breaking up of his castled position.

However, White finds a way to make his advantage tell.

	15 Q–N5ch	K–R1
	16 Q–B6ch	K–N1
	17 N–Q5	Q–Q1
	18 N–K7ch	Resigns

Black must give up his Queen for the Knight. After 18 ...

QxN; **19** QxQ, White would win very quickly because of his material advantage and the exposed position of Black's King.

This last game should be played over very carefully because it gives the student a good insight into the problems of attack and defence.

All the games in this chapter have been selected to illustrate certain points.

The games show the power of attacks based on check. The games emphasize the importance of developing rapidly. They show how a failure to castle can lead to disaster.

But more, the games also present a positive moral. They show you economical and efficient methods of development. They show you how to exploit the mistakes of your opponent. They give you valuable principles and techniques to apply in your own games.

PART II
The Openings

THE OPENINGS

The opening is in many ways the most crucial point of a game of chess. Most players are reasonably content with their middle game and end game play. The part that worries them is the opening. And this with good reason.

For the opening determines the course of the later play. A careless move, a poor plan, a negligent development—all these are factors that may ruin your game from the very start.

Another difficulty about opening play is the great multiplicity of openings and opening play. How can the average player see the woods for the trees? The object of this guide to the openings is to classify them in orderly fashion, to give you a clear view of the chief lines of play and the recommended procedures.

Careful study of this section will greatly reduce confusion and give the student a clarifying introduction to this vastly ramified subject. *Better opening play means better results in your games!*

5. KING PAWN OPENINGS

CENTRE GAME

	1	P–K4	P–K4
	2	P–Q4	PxP
	3	QxP	N–QB3

DIAGRAM 60
(*White to move*)
Black has the initiative because he gains time attacking the Queen

This opening is rarely seen nowadays because White's early development of the Queen allows Black to develop with gain of time.

A likely continuation is 4 Q–K3, N–B3; 5 N–QB3, B–N5;

6 B–Q2, Castles; 7 Castles, R–K1 with a very promising game for Black.

DANISH GAMBIT

1	P–K4	P–K4
2	P–Q4	PxP
3	P–QB3	...

DIAGRAM 61

(*Black to move*)

White is about to offer two Pawns for a speculative attack

3	...	PxP

If Black wants to play it safe, his most prudent course is 3 . . . P–Q4!; 4 KPxP, N–KB3! favouring development ahead of material.

4	B–QB4	PxP
5	BxP	P–QB3

After 6 N–QB3, P–Q3; 7 N–B3, N–Q2!; 8 Castles, N–B4! Black has a cramped but tenacious defensive position.

BISHOP'S OPENING

1	P–K4	P–K4
2	B–B4	N–KB3

DIAGRAM 62

(*White to move*)

Black counter attacks with gain of time

3	P–Q3	P–B3!
4	P–B4	PxP
5	QBxP	P–Q4
6	PxP	NxP

Black is on the way to achieving a satisfactory development.

VIENNA GAME

| 1 | P–K4 | P–K4 |
| 2 | N–QB3 | N–KB3 |

DIAGRAM 63

(*White to move*)

White can choose between advancing his King Bishop Pawn at once or later on

White's two main lines are:

3 B–B4, N–B3; 4 P–Q3, B–N5; 5 B–N5, P–KR3; 6 BxN, BxNch; 7 PxB, QxB; 8 N–K2 followed by 9 Castles.

3 P–B4, P–Q4!; 4 BPxP, NxP; 5 N–B3, B–K2; 6 P–Q4, Castles; 7 B–Q3, P–KB4!

In either case the players have equal prospects.

KING'S BISHOP'S GAMBIT

1	P–K4	P–K4
2	P–KB4	PxP
3	B–B4	. . .

DIAGRAM 64

(*Black to move*)

Black plays for quick and effective development, even at the cost of a Pawn

3	. . .	N–KB3!
4	N–QB3	P–B3!
5	Q–B3	P–Q4!

And after 6 PxP, B–Q3!; 7 P–Q3, B–KN5!; 8 Q–B2, Castles! Black has a clear initiative.

KING'S KNIGHT'S GAMBIT

1	P–K4	P–K4
2	P–KB4	PxP
3	N–KB3	. . .

DIAGRAM 65
(*Black to move*)
Black will play to hold on to the gambit Pawn

A likely continuation is: 3 ... P–KN4; 4 B–B4, B–N2; 5 Castles, P–Q3; 6 P–Q4, P–KR3; 7 P–B3, N–K2; 8 P–KN3, P–N5; 9 N–R4, P–B6; 10 B–B4, B–K3. White has an imposing Pawn centre, while Black has retained his advantage of a Pawn.

KIESERITZKY GAMBIT

1	P–K4	P–K4
2	P–KB4	PxP
3	N–KB3	P–KN4
4	P–KR3	P–N5
5	N–K5	. . .

DIAGRAM 66
(*Black to move*)
White's attempt to break up Black's King-side Pawn formation is not destined to succeed

After 5 . . . N–KB3!; 6 B–B4, P–Q4!; 7 PxP, B–N2; 8 P–Q4,
N–R4! we find that Black has a very strong game. Returning
the extra Pawn often pays dividends for the gambit defender.

KING'S GAMBIT DECLINED

1	P–K4	P–K4
2	P–KB4	B–B4

DIAGRAM 67

(*White to move*)

**Note this trap: if 3 PxP???, Q-R5ch
forces mate or wins a Rook!**

3	N–KB3	P–Q3
4	B–B4	N–KB3
5	N–B3	N–B3
6	P–Q3	B–K3!

Black stands well after 7 BxB, PxB; or 7 B–N5, P–QR3;
8 BxNch, PxB; 9 P–B5, B–B1.

FALKBEER COUNTER GAMBIT

1	P–K4	P–K4
2	P–KB4	P–Q4?!

DIAGRAM 68

(*White to move*)

**Black's early counter attack looks
premature**

3	KPxP	P–K5

Black's idea is to make it awkward for White to develop his
pieces. However, after 4 P–Q3!, N–KB3; 5 Q–K2!, QxP;

6 N–QB3, B–QN5; 7 B–Q2, BxN; 8 BxB White stands to come out a Pawn ahead, without in any way endangering his position.

GRECO COUNTER GAMBIT

1	P–K4	P–K4
2	N–KB3	P–KB4

DIAGRAM 69

(White to move)

White will succeed in repulsing Black's premature counter attack

3	NxP!	Q–B3
4	P–Q4	P–Q3
5	N–B4	PxP

After 6 N–B3, Q–N3; 7 B–B4, N–KB3; 8 N–K3, B–K2; 9 B–B4, P–B3; 10 P–Q5! Black has difficulty developing his pieces. The violent counterthrust 10 ... P–N4; 11 B–QN3, P–N5; 12 N–R4, P–B4 allows 13 P–QR3! with favourable line-opening for White

PHILIDOR'S DEFENCE

1	P–K4	P–K4
2	N–KB3	P–Q3
3	P–Q4!	...

DIAGRAM 70

(White to move)

Black's last move condemns him to a cramped position

If Black surrenders the centre with 3 ... PxP White has a

much freer game after 4 QxP!, N–QB3; 5 B–QN5!, B–Q2; 6 BxN, BxB; 7 N–B3, N–B3; 8 B–N5, etc.

Holding the centre also gives a dreary game for Black: 3 . . . N–Q2; 4 B–QB4, P–QB3; 5 N–B3, B–K2; 6 PxP, PxP; 7 N–KN5!, BxN; 8 Q–R5! (threatens mate), Q–B3; 9 BxB, Q–N3; 10 Q–R4, etc.

PETROFF'S DEFENCE

| 1 | P–K4 | P–K4 |
| 2 | N–KB3 | N–KB3 |

DIAGRAM 71
(White to move)
White must play energetically to repulse the counter attack

White must fight back hard to maintain the initiative, for example: 3 NxP, P–Q3; 4 N–KB3, NxP; 5 P–Q4, P–Q4; 6 B–Q3, B–Q3; 7 Castles, Castles; 8 P–B4!, B–KN5; 9 PxP, P–KB4?!; 10 N–B3!, N–Q2?!; 11 P–KR3!, B–R4; 12 NxN, PxN; 13 BxP, N–B3; 14 B–B5!, K–R1; 15 P–KN4!, NxQP?!; 16 B–K6!, B–B2; 17 N–N5, BxB; 18 NxB, Q–R5; 19 Q–N3! and White wins!

SCOTCH GAME

1	P–K4	P–K4
2	N–KB3	N–QB3
3	P–Q4	PxP
4	NxP	. . .

DIAGRAM 72
(Black to move)
White has lost time by moving his King Knight twice

Black has an easy game after 4 ... B–B4; 5 B–K3, Q–B3; 6 P–QB3, KN–K2; 7 B–QN5, Castles; 8 Castles, P–Q3; 9 NxN, PxN; 10 BxB, BPxB; or 4 ... N–B3; 5 N–QB3, B–N5; 6 NxN, PxN; 7 B–Q3, P–Q4!

PONZIANI OPENING

1	P–K4	P–K4
2	N–KB3	N–QB3
3	P–B3	...

DIAGRAM 73

(Black to move)

White's last move pre-empts the best square for his Queen Knight

Black has easy equality with 3 ... N–B3!; 4 P–Q4, P–Q4!

If then 5 B–QN5, KPxP; 6 NxP, B–Q2; 7 PxP, NxN; 8 BxBch, QxB; 9 QxN, QxP with placid equality.

Or 5 KPxP, QxP; 6 B–K2, P–K5; 7 KN–Q2, P–K6!; 8 PxP, QxNP; 9 B–B3, Q–R6 and White's King is unsafe.

HUNGARIAN DEFENCE

1	P–K4	P–K4
2	N–KB3	N–QB3
3	B–B4	B–K2

DIAGRAM 74

(White to move)

Black's last move gives him a very constricted position

| 4 | P–Q4 | P–Q3 |

White now ties up Black's pieces badly with 5 P–Q5!, N–N1; 6 B–Q3!, N–KB3; 7 P–B4, Castles; 8 P–KR3!, P–B3; 9 N–B3, N–K1; 10 P–KN4! preventing the freeing move ... P–KB4. White has an enormous advantage in mobility.

GIUOCO PIANO

1	P–K4	P–K4
2	N–KB3	N–QB3
3	B–B4	B–B4

DIAGRAM 75
(*White to move*)
White has a choice of several plans

If White decides to form a Pawn centre with P–B3 and P–Q4, the following is a likely possibility: 4 P–B3, N–B3; 5 P–Q4, PxP; 6 PxP, B–N5ch; 7 N–B3!?, NxKP; 8 Castles. Now Black plays it safe, avoiding further Pawn captures, thus: 8 ... BxN; 9 P–Q5!?, N–K4; 10 PxB, NxB; 11 Q–Q4, P–KB4! Again the safest; after 12 QxN/B4, P–Q3 Black has a good game, with a Pawn ahead.

Black can also hold the centre, after 4 P–B3, by playing 4 ... Q–K2 and if 5 P–Q4, B–N3. But in that case Black's position is rather cramped after 6 Castles, N–B3; 7 R–K1, P–Q3; 8 P–KR3!, Castles; 9 N–R3!, N–Q1; 10 B–Q3, P–B4; 11 N–B4, B–B2; 12 PxKP!, PxP; 13 N–K3!

White can also play his Queen Pawn to Queen 3. This leads to a quiet, conservative game, for example 4 P–Q3, N–B3; 5 N–B3, P–Q3; 6 B–K3, B–N3. Or 5 P–B3, P–Q3; 6 QN–Q2, Castles; etc.

EVANS GAMBIT

1	P–K4	P–K4
2	N–KB3	N–QB3
3	B–B4	B–B4
4	P–QN4	. . .

DIAGRAM 76
(Black to move)
White offers a Pawn to gain time for development

If the Pawn is accepted, White gets a powerful Pawn centre and a commanding lead in development: 4 . . . BxNP; 5 P–B3, B–B4; 6 P–Q4, PxP; 7 PxP, B–N3; 8 Castles, P–Q3; 9 N–B3, etc.

Safer is 4 . . . B–N3!; 5 P–QR4, P–QR3; 6 B–N2, P–Q3 and Black has an excellent game.

TWO KNIGHTS' DEFENCE

	1	P–K4	P–K4
	2	N–KB3	N–QB3
	3	B–B4	N–B3

DIAGRAM 77
(White to move)
White can either win a Pawn or sacrifice a Pawn

After 4 N–N5, P–Q4; 5 PxP Black's best course is 5 . . . N–QR4. Then after 6 B–N5ch, P–B3; 7 PxP, PxP; 8 B–K2, P–KR3; 9 N–KB3, P–K5; 10 N–K5, B–Q3 Black has a good development in return for the Pawn.

If instead of 4 P–Q4, PxP; 5 Castles, NxP; 6 R–K1, P–Q4; 7 BxP!, QxB; 8 N–B3!, Q–QR4; 9 NxN, B–K3 the position is about even.

FOUR KNIGHTS' GAME

	1	P–K4	P–K4
	2	N–KB3	N–QB3
	3	N–B3	N–B3

DIAGRAM 78
(White to move)
An opening that leads to heavy manœuvring play

Black can hold his own after 4 B–N5, B–N5; 5 Castles, Castles; 6 P–Q3, P–Q3; 7 B–N5, N–K2; 8 BxN, PxB; 9 N–KR4, N–N3; 10 NxN, RPxN.

The same is true after Black branches off with 6 ... BxN; 7 PxB, P–Q3. For example: 8 B–N5, Q–K2 and Black's position is quite solid.

RUY LOPEZ

1	P–K4	P–K4
2	N–KB3	N–QB3
3	B–N5	...

DIAGRAM 79
(Black to move)
Many authorities consider this the strongest opening at White's disposal

Black has a great many alternative defences at his disposal. Let us consider some of them.

The most popular is 3 ... P–QR3, for example; 4 B–R4, N–B3; 5 Castles, B–K2. This is known as the " Strong Point Defence," and continues along these lines: 6 R–K1, P–QN4; 7 B–N3, P–Q3; 8 P–B3, N–QR4; 9 B–B2, P–B4; 10 P–Q4, Q–B2. Black plays to maintain his Pawn set-up intact. A plausible sequel is 11 P–KR3, Castles; 12 QN–Q2, N–Q2; 13 N–B1, N–N3; 14 P–QN3, N–B3; 15 P–Q5, N–Q1; 16 P–KN4, P–B3. Black's position is very hard to break through.

A totally different kind of game comes about after 3 ...
P–QR3; 4 B–R4, N–B3; 5 Castles, NxP. Known as the "Open
Defence," this continues 6 P–Q4, P–QN4; 7 B–N3, P–Q4;
8 PxP, B–K3. A likely follow-up is the following: 9 P–B3,
B–K2; 10 QN–Q2, Castles; 11 Q–K2, N–B4; 12 N–Q4, NxB;
13 QNxN, Q–Q2; 14 NxN, QxN; 15 B–K3, B–KB4 with even
prospects.

Still another possibility after 3 ... P–QR3; 4 B–R4 is 4 ...
P–Q3. One of the most popular continuations is 5 BxNch,
PxB; 6 P–Q4, P–B3; 7 B–K3, P–N3; 8 Q–Q2, N–K2; 9 N–B3,
B–KN2. In that case White's position is somewhat freer while
Black has the two Bishops.

Coming back to Diagram 79, there are other variations to
be considered. There is for instance the "Berlin Defence":
3 ... N–B3; 4 Castles, NxP; 5 P–Q4, B–K2; 6 Q–K2, N–Q3;
7 BxN, NPxB; 8 PxP, N–N2. Again Black has the two Bishops,
but his development is awkward. White has the better game
here.

Another line to be considered is the "Steinitz Defence."
This proceeds with 3 ... P–Q3, and a popular continuation is
4 P–Q4, B–Q2; 5 N–B3, N–B3; 6 BxN, BxB; 7 Q–Q3, PxP;
8 NxP with a noticeably freer game for White.

FRENCH DEFENCE

	1	P–K4	P–K3
	2	P–Q4	P–Q4

DIAGRAM 80

(*White to move*)

This is a defence that is at once conservative and yet possessed of great fighting qualities

White can at once provoke a crisis by advancing boldly in
the centre with 3 P–K5, to which the best answer is counter
attack by 3 ... P–QB4! Then after 4 P–QB3, N–QB3; 5 N–B3,
Q–N3; 6 B–Q3, PxP; 7 PxP, B–Q2; 8 B–K2, KN–K2; 9 P–QN3,
N–B4; 10 B–N2, B–N5ch with a fighting game in which both
sides have chances.

In the position of Diagram 80 White can guard his King Pawn with 3 N–Q2. In that case he gets a slightly better endgame after 3 . . . P–QB4; 4 KPxP, KPxP; 5 B–N5ch, B–Q2; 6 Q–K2ch, Q–K2; 7 BxBch, NxB; 8 PxP, QxQch; 9 NxQ, BxP; 10 QN–N3, B–N3; 11 QN–Q4, KN–B3. Perhaps Black's freedom of action is enough compensation for his isolated Queen Pawn.

Another way for White to guard his King Pawn in the position of Diagram 80 is 3 N–QB3. Then if Black counter attacks with 3 B–N5 there may follow 4 P–K5, P–QB4; 5 P–QR3, BxNch; 6 PxB, N–K2. In that case White has a very aggressive position after 7 Q–N4, N–B4; 8 N–B3, P–KR4; 9 Q–B4, etc.

Going back to the position of Diagram 80, the usual reply to 3 N–QB3 is 3 . . . N–KB3. Then after 4 B–KN5, B–N5 we may get the following: 5 P–K5, P–KR3 (forced); 6 B–Q2, BxN; 7 PxB, N–K5; 8 Q–N4, P–KN3; 9 B–B1! White sacrifices a Pawn in order to hold on to his strong Bishop, and after 9 . . . NxQBP; 10 B–Q3 he has an aggressive position.

Another sacrifice arises after 3 N–QB3, N–KB3; 4 B–KN5, B–K2; 5 P–K5, KN–Q2; 6 P–KR4! If Black plays 6 . . . BxB?; 7 PxB, QxP; 8 N–R3, Q–K2 White's initiative is too powerful after 9 Q–N4. Therefore Black continues in safer fashion with 6 . . . P–QB4!; 7 BxB, KxB!; 8 P–B4, PxP; 9 QxP, N–QB3; 10 Q–Q2, P–QR3 when the position is fairly even.

SICILIAN DEFENCE

    1 P–K4   P–QB4

DIAGRAM 81

(*White to move*)

One of the most aggressive as well as riskiest defences in reply to 1 P–K4

White has many systems at his disposal in answer to this defence. For example: 2 N–QB3, N–QB3; 3 P–KN3, P–KN3; 4 B–N2, B–N2; 5 KN–K2, P–K3; 6 Castles, KN–K2; 7 P–Q3, Castles; 8 B–K3, N–Q5! with a promising position for both sides.

The usual procedure is:

    2 N–KB3

If now 2 . . . P–K3; 3 P–Q4, PxP; 4 NxP, N–KB3; 5 N–QB3, N–B3; 6 N/Q4–N5, B–N5; 7 P–QR3, BxNch; 8 NxB, P–Q4; 9 PxP, PxP; 10 B–Q3 with White for choice. He has two Bishops and Black has an isolated Queen Pawn.

2	. . .	N–QB3
3	P–Q4	PxP
4	NxP	N–B3
5	N–QB3	P–Q3
6	B–K2	. . .

Here we branch off, depending on whether or not Black wants to fianchetto his King Bishop. After 6 . . . P–KN3; 7 B–K3, B–N2; 8 Castles, Castles; 9 N–N3, B–K3; 10 P–B4, B–K3; 11 P–B5, B–B5! a sharp fighting game is in prospect.

On the other hand, after 6 . . . P–K3 the sequel might be: 7 Castles, B–K2; 8 B–K3, P–QR3; 9 P–QR4, Q–B2; 10 N–N3, P–QN3; 11 P–B4, Castles! 12 B–B3, B–N2; 13 Q–K1. White intends a Kingside attack against Black's position, which is cramped but sturdy.

CARRO-KANN DEFENCE

1	P–K4	P–QB3

DIAGRAM 82
(*White to move*)
This defence is solid as well as stolid

It is usual for White to advance his Queen Pawn immediately, but this is not absolutely essential, for example: 2 N–QB3, P–Q4; 3 N–B3, P–Q5?; 4 N–K2, P–QB4; 5 P–B3 forcing Black to give up the centre by 5 . . . PxP.

2	P–Q4	P–Q4

White's chief continuation is 3 N–QB3, for example 3 . . . PxP; 4 NxP, B–B4; 5 N–N3, B–N3; 6 P–KR4, P–KR3; 7 N–B3, N–Q2; 8 P–R5, B–R2; 9 B–Q3, BxB; 10 QxB, KN–B3; 11 B–Q2, P–K3; 12 Castles(Q), Q–B2; 13 K–N1, Castles; 14 P–B4, P–B4; 15 B–B3 and White enjoys slightly more freedom.

After 3 N–QB3, PxP; 4 NxP Black may challenge White's centralized Knight with 4 . . . N–B3. A likely continuation is 5 NxNch, KPxN; 6 B–QB4, B–K2; 7 Q–R5, Castles; 8 N–K2, B–K3; 9 B–Q3, P–KR3. White has the positional advantage of the Queen-side majority of Pawns and his position is freer.

Another line of play after 2 . . . P–Q4 starts with 3 PxP, PxP; 4 P–QB4. Then, after 4 . . . N–KB3; 5 N–QB3, P–K3!; 6 B–N5, B–K2; 7 N–B3, Castles; 8 B–Q3, PxP; 9 BxP, QN–Q2; 10 Castles, N–N3; 11 B–N3, QN–Q4 Black seems to have a fairly solid game and White's isolated Queen Pawn is a potential end game weakness.

ALEKHINE'S DEFENCE

<table>
<tr><td>1 P–K4</td><td>N–KB3</td></tr>
</table>

DIAGRAM 83
(*White to move*)
A daring defence—perhaps too daring

Black wants to tempt the advance of White's centre Pawns in the hope of thereupon stamping them as weaknesses. This policy fails more often than it succeeds.

<table>
<tr><td>2 P–K5</td><td>N–Q4</td></tr>
</table>

White can now proceed in quiet, reasonable fashion with 3 P–Q4, P–Q3; 4 N–KB3, B–N5; 5 B–K2, P–QB3; 6 N–N5!, B–B4; 7 B–Q3, BxB; 8 QxB, P–KR3; 9 N–KB3, P–K3; 10 Castles, PxP; 11 PxP, N–Q2; 12 R–Q1, Q–B2. This leaves White with a substantially more active position after 13 Q–K2.

<table>
<tr><td>3 P–QB4</td><td>N–N3</td></tr>
<tr><td>4 P–Q4</td><td>P–Q3</td></tr>
<tr><td>5 P–B4</td><td>. . .</td></tr>
</table>

This is White's boldest course. After 5 . . . PxP; 6 BPxP, N–B3; 7 B–K3, B–B4; 8 N–QB3, P–K3; 9 N–B3, Q–Q2; 10 B–K2, Castles; 11 Castles, P–B3; 12 PxP, PxP White has much greater freedom of action.

One interesting possibility is the following: 13 P–Q5, N–K4; 14 BxN, NxNch; 15 BxN, BPxB; 16 P–QR3!, B–B4ch; 17 K–R1, P–K4; 18 P–QN4, B–Q5; 19 N–N5!, BxR; 20 NxPch, K–N1; 21 N–N5 with the winning threat of Q–R4.

CENTRE COUNTER GAME

<table>
<tr><td>1</td><td>P–K4</td><td>P–Q4</td></tr>
</table>

DIAGRAM 84

(*White to move*)

A faulty defence because it loses time for black

<table>
<tr><td>2</td><td>PxP</td><td>QxP</td></tr>
<tr><td>3</td><td>N–QB3</td><td>Q–QR4</td></tr>
</table>

This is Black's most aggressive continuation. After 4 P–Q4 his best line is probably 4 . . . N–KB3; 5 N–B3, B–N5; 6 B–K2, N–B3; 7 B–K3, Castles; 8 N–Q2!, BxB; 9 QxB!, Q–KB4; 10 N–N3, P–K3.

White stands better. After Castling on the Queen-side, he will threaten N–R4 and N–B5 followed by Q–N5. Black's development is somewhat backward.

6. QUEEN PAWN OPENINGS

QUEEN'S GAMBIT DECLINED (... P–K3)

1	P–Q4	P–Q4
2	P–QB4	P–K3

DIAGRAM 85

(*White to move*)

An opening in which Black often has trouble developing his Queen Bishop

3	N–QB3	N–KB3

If now 4 N–B3, P–B4! and Black can achieve equality, for example 5 P–K3, N–B3 with a symmetrical position. 5 BPxP, NxP!; 6 P–K4, NxN; 7 PxN, PxP; 8 PxP, B–N5ch!; 9 B–Q2, BxBch; 10 QxB, Castles; 11 B–B4, N–B3; 12 Castles, P–QN3; 13 KR–Q1, B–N2 involves much more complicated play, but it leads to a fairly level game. White's Pawn centre is impressive, but Black's majority of Pawns on the Queen-side gives him good endgame prospects.

4	B–N5	...

Black can now simplify, if he is so minded, by playing 4 ... B–K2; 5 P–K3, Castles; 6 N–B3, P–KR3; 7 B–R4, N–K5!; 8 BxB, QxB; 9 PxP, NxN; 10 PxN, PxP. In that event Black has freed his game considerably and has nothing to fear, for example: 11 Q–N3, Q–Q3; 12 P–B4, PxP; 13 BxP, N–B3!; 14 Q–B3, B–N5. Black's development is notably aggressive.

4	...	QN–Q2
5	P–K3	P–B3

White can play 6 N–B3, and if Black replies 6 ... Q–R4 we have the "Cambridge Springs Variation." There might follow 7 N–Q2 (to unpin his other Knight), PxP; 8 BxN, NxB;

9 NxP, Q–B2 and it is a moot point whether Black's two Bishops outweigh his rather cramped position.

Still another possibility is 6 N–B3, B–K2; 7 R–B1, Castles; 8 B–Q3, PxP and Black starts a number of exchanges to obtain freedom. However, after 9 BxP, N–Q4; 10 BxB, QxB; 11 Castles, NxN; 12 RxN, P–K4 we conclude that White's game is preferable.

6   PxP   . . .

This move, based on rather a subtle idea, constitutes the " Exchange Variation." After 6 . . . KPxP; 7 B–Q3, B–K2; 8 Q–B2!, Castles; 9 N–B3, R–K1; 10 Castles KR, N–B1; 11 QR–N1! White enjoys appreciably more freedom and threatens to play P–QN4 and P–QN5 with a view to opening a file on the Queen-side.

Before we leave this opening, let us take another look at Diagram 85 and consider this variation: 3 N–QB3, P–QB4; 4 BPxP!, KPxP; 5 N–B3, N–QB3; 6 P–KN3!; N–B3, 7 B–N2, B–K2; 8 Castles, Castles; 9 PxP!, BxP. White's fianchettoed Bishop is powerfully trained on Black's isolated Queen Pawn. Black is in trouble, despite his excellent development.

In general, it may be said of this opening that it calls for exceptionally skilled positional judgment.

QUEEN'S GAMBIT DECLINED (. . . P–QB3)

1   P–Q4   P–Q4
2   P–QB4   P–QB3

DIAGRAM 86

(White to move)

This defence has the advantage of allowing the early development of Black's Queen Bishop in some variations

White can exchange Pawns in the centre, but this permits Black to hold his own: 3 PxP, PxP; 4 N–QB3, N–KB3; 5 N–B3, N–B3; 6 B–B4, B–B4!; 7 P–K3, P–K3; 8 Q–N3, B–QN5! and now if 9 B–QN5, Castles!; 10 BxN, BxNch; 11 QxB, R–B1!

3 N–KB3   N–B3

White can, if he wishes, now defend his Queen Bishop Pawn with 4 P–K3. In that case 4 . . . B–B4; 5 B–Q3, BxB; 6 QxB, P–K3; 7 N–B3, QN–Q2 leads to a fairly level game.

4 N–B3   . . .

Black must now choose between 4 . . . PxP, leaving open the possibility of developing by . . . B–B4—and 4 . . . P–K3, which blocks in the Bishop.

After 4 . . . P–K3 the lively and risky "Meran Defence" may be in the cards: 5 P–K3, QN–Q2; 6 B–Q3, PxP; 7 BxBP, P–QN4; 8 B–Q3, P–QR3; 9 P–K4!, P–B4!; 10 P–K5, PxP!; 11 NxNP, NxP!; 12 NxN, PxN; 13 Q–B3, B–N5ch!; 14 K–K2, QR–N1; 15 Q–N3, Q–Q3! with about equal chances.

On the other hand, after 4 . . . P–K3; 5 P–K3, QN–Q2; 6 B–Q3, B–Q3; 7 Castles, Castles; 8 P–K4!, PxKP; 9 NxP, NxN; 10 BxN White has much greater freedom of action because both of his Bishops are on open diagonals.

The most exciting line is 4 . . . P–K3; 5 B–N5!? (the "Anti-Meran Defence"), PxP; 6 P–K4, P–N4; 7 P–K5, P–KR3; 8 B–R4, P–N4; 9 NxKNP!, PxN; 10 BxNP, QN–Q2 with very unclear play.

4 . . .   PxP
5 P–QR4   B–B4

Now Black has the development he wanted. Nevertheless, White can maintain a certain amount of advantage by 6 P–K3, P–K3; 7 BxP, B–QN5; 8 Castles, Castles; 9 Q–K2 (threatening P–K4). Thus if 9 . . . B–N5; 10 P–R3, BxN; 11 QxB, QN–Q2; 12 R–Q1, P–K4; 13 P–Q5! White has some initiative. And if 9 . . . N–K5 the Pawn sacrifice 10 B–Q3! gives Black a difficult game: 10 . . . BxN; 11 PxB!, NxQBP; 12 Q–B2, BxB; 13 QxB, N–Q4; 14 B–R3. White's magnificent position is well worth a Pawn.

Also possible is 6 N–K5, QN–Q2; 7 NxP/B4, Q–B2; 8 P–KN3!, P–K4; 9 PxP; NxP; 10 B–B4, KN–Q2; 11 B–N2, P–B3; 12 Castles, R–Q1; 13 Q–B1! and Black's game is uncomfortable.

Thus we see that the chance of developing by . . . B–B4 in this opening is not an unmixed blessing.

QUEEN'S GAMBIT ACCEPTED

1 P–Q4   P–Q4
2 P–QB4   PxP

DIAGRAM 87
(*White to move*)
Black accepts the gambit Pawn

3   N–KB3   . . .

An interesting divergence from the main line is now 3 . . .
P–QR3; 4 P–K3, B–N5. But after 5 BxP, P–K3; 6 P–KR3,
B–R4; 7 Q–N3!, BxN; 8 PxB, P–QN4; 9 B–K2 White is better
off because he has the two Bishops and the open King Knight file.

3	. . .	N–KB3	6	Castles	P–QR3
4	P–K3	P–K3	7	Q–K2	N–B3
5	BxP	P–B4			

White can now continue simply and forcefully with 8 PxP!,
BxP; 9 P–QR3!, P–QN4; 10 B–R2, B–N2; 11 P–QN4, B–K2;
12 B–N2, Castles; 13 QN–Q2!, Q–N3; 14 N–N3, KR–Q1; 15
QR–B1, QR–B1; 16 N–B5 with marked positional advantage.

8	R–Q1	P–QN4	10	B–Q3	BxP
9	PxP!	Q–B2	11	P–QR4!	P–N5

And after 12 QN–Q2, Castles; 13 N–N3, B–K2; 14 P–K4!
White has an excellent game.

ALBIN COUNTER GAMBIT

1	P–Q4	P–Q4
2	P–QB4	P–K4?!

DIAGRAM 88
(*White to move*)
**Black's intended Pawn sacrifice of a
Pawn is unsound**

3 QPxP   P–Q5

This is played to block White's development. However, the counter gambit should not work because Black either remains a Pawn down or loses too much time regaining it. A likely continuation is 4 N–KB3, N–QB3; 5 P–KN3, B–K3; 6 QN–Q2, Q–Q2; 7 B–N2, R–Q1; 8 Castles, KN–K2; 9 Q–R4, N–N3; 10 P–QR3, B–K2; 11 P–QN4, Castles; 12 B–N2 and White has all the play.

COLLE SYSTEM

1	P–Q4	P–Q4
2	N–KB3	N–KB3
3	P–K3	P–B4
4	P–B3	. . .

DIAGRAM 89
(*Black to move*)
Black equalizes with little trouble

Black can obtain equality in several ways, for example: 4 . . . P–K3; 5 QN–Q2, QN–Q2!; 6 B–Q3, B–Q3; 7 Castles, Castles; 8 R–K1, Q–N3!

Another way is 4 . . . P–KN3; 5 QN–Q2, QN–Q2; 6 B–Q3, B–N2; 7 Castles, Castles; 8 P–K4, QPxP; 9 NxP, PxP; 10 NxP, etc.

NIMZOINDIAN DEFENCE

DIAGRAM 90
(*White to move*)
Black's pin prevents White from playing P–K4

1	P–Q4	N–KB3
2	P–QB4	P–K3
3	N–QB3	B–N5

White has a number of systems of development at his disposal. One is 4 P–QR3 (the sharpest), BxNch; 5 PxB, P–B4; 6 P–B3, P–Q3; 7 P–K4, N–B3; 8 B–K3, P–K4; 9 P–Q5, N–QR4; 10 B–Q3, Castles; 11 N–K2 with a difficult and complicated game.

One of the quietest but most effective lines against the Nimzoindian Defence is 4 P–K3, for example 4 . . . P–Q4; 5 B–Q3, Castles; 6 N–K2, P–B4; 7 Castles, N–B3; 8 BPxP, KPxP; 9 PxP, BxP; 10 P–QR3, N–K4; 11 B–B2, P–QR4. White has a strong outpost for his Knights at Queen 4 and he has substantial pressure against Black's isolated Pawn.

White can also resort to Queen moves, for example 4 Q–N3, N–B3; 5 N–B3, N–K5; 6 P–QR3, BxNch; 7 PxB, P–B4; 8 P–K3, Castles. This leads to about an even game. White has prospects for his two Bishops with B–Q3 and P–QR4 followed by B–R3; Black, on the other hand, can advance in the centre with . . . P–Q3 and . . . P–K4.

White's' most promising line is perhaps 4 Q–B2, with this continuation: 4 . . . P–Q4; 5 PxP, QxP; 6 P–K3, P–B4; 7 B–Q2, BxN; 8 BxB, PxP; 9 NxP, P–K4; 10 N–B3, N–B3; 11 P–K3, Castles; 12 B–K2, B–N5. The two Bishops at White's disposal give somewhat the better prospects. On the other hand, Black has developed freely and rapidly.

QUEEN'S INDIAN DEFENCE

1	P–Q4	N–KB3
2	P–QB4	P–K3
3	N–KB3	P–QN3

DIAGRAM 91

(*White to move*)

White fights for control of the long diagonal by fianchettoing his own Bishop

After 4 P–KN3!, B–N2; 5 B–N2 White's prospects are better, for example: 5 . . . B–N5ch; 6 B–Q2, BxBch; 7 QxB!, Castles; 8 N–B3, P–Q3; 9 Q–B2 followed by 10 P–K4 with a strong position. Or 5 . . . B–K2; 6 Castles, Castles; 7 N–B3, N–K5; 8 Q–B2, NxN; 9 QxN, P–KB4; 10 N–K1, BxB; 11 NxB and White's position is more comfortable.

KING'S INDIAN DEFENCE

1	P–Q4	N–KB3
2	P–QB4	P–KN3

DIAGRAM 92
(White to move)
In this opening Black always fianchettoes his King Bishop, and White often follows suit

White can now play 3 N–QB3, B–N2; 4 P–K4, Castles; 5 B–K2, QN–Q2; 6 Castles, P–K4; 7 R–K1 with a good game. However, the more usual course is:

3	P–KN3	B–N2
4	B–N2	. . .

Black can try 4 . . . P–Q4 here, but this usually gives White a great preponderance in the centre, for example: 4 . . . P–Q4; 5 PxP, NxP; 6 P–K4!, N–N3; 7 N–K2, Castles; 8 Castles, N–B3; 9 P–Q5, N–N1; 10 QN–B3 and White monopolizes the centre.

4	. . .	P–Q3
5	P–K4	Castles
6	N–K2	P–K4

White can now push by: 7 P–Q5, P–QR4!, 8 Castles, QN–Q2; 9 QN–B3, N–B4; 10 P–KR3, N–K1; 11 B–K3 with a good game.

Another way is:

7	Castles	QN–Q2
8	QN–B3	PxP
9	NxP	P–B3
10	P–KR3!	N–N3

White's position is very strong, for example 11 P–N3, P–Q4; 12 KPxP, PxP; 13 B–R3!, R–K1; 14 P–B5! driving Black back all along the line.

GRUENFELD DEFENCE

1	P–Q4	N–KB3
2	P–QB4	P–KN3
3	N–QB3	P–Q4

DIAGRAM 93

(White to move)

Black combines the fianchetto with the advance of his Queen Pawn

White has many alternative ways of proceeding, for example: 4 P–K3, B–N2; 5 Q–N3, P–B3; 6 N–B3, Castles; 7 B–Q2, P–K3. White's position is more comfortable after 8 B–Q3, QN–Q2; 9 Castles, P–N3; 10 PxP, KPxP; 11 P–K4, PxP; 12 NxP, P–B4!; 13 NxNch, NxN; 14 PxP, PxP; 15 KR–Q1.

Another possibility is 4 PxP, NxP; 5 P–K4, NxN; 6 PxN, P–QB4; 7 B–N5ch, B–Q2; 8 B–QB4, B–N2; 9 N–K2, PxP; 10 PxP. Castles; 11 Castles, N–B3; 12 B–K3, R–B1!; 13 R–B1, N–R4; 14 B–Q3, P–QN4! with a view to . . . N–B5. Despite White's imposing Pawn centre, Black has a good counter pressure.

White's strongest line may well be 4 N–B3, B–N2; 5 Q–N3. After 5 . . . PxP; 6 QxBP, Castles; 7 P–K4, B–N5; 8 B–K3, N/B3–Q2; 9 Q–N3, N–N3; 10 R–Q1, N–B3; 11 P–Q5, N–K4; 12 B–K2 Black's position is very crowded and White has all the play.

On the other hand, 4 B–B4, B–N2; 5 P–K3, Castles!; 6 Q–N3, P–B4!; 7 QPxP, N–K5; 8 PxP is too greedy. After 8 . . . Q–R4;

9 N–K2, NxQBP; 10 Q–B4, P–K4! Black has a very powerful position. White does well, therefore, to avoid this dangerous variation.

BUDAPEST DEFENCE

1	P–Q4	N–KB3
2	P–QB4	P–K4!?

DIAGRAM 94
(White to move)
White's best method of handling this gambit is to avoid material gain

3	PxP	...

A curious reply sometimes adopted by Black at this point is 3 . . . N–K5. White's best course is to continue 4 N–KB3, N–QB3; 5 QN–Q2, N–B4; 6 P–KN3, allowing Black to regain his Pawn by 6 . . . Q–K2 with considerable loss of time. Or, if Black prefers a true gambit with 6 . . . P–Q3; 7 PxP, QxP White still stubbornly offers back the extra Pawn with 8 B–N2, B–B4; 9 P–QR3, P–QR4; 10 Castles, Castles; 11 P–QN4! in return for a powerful attack.

3	...	N–N5

The normal move. White's most natural reply is 4 P–K4, with the following likely continuation: 4 . . . NxKP; 5 P–B4, KN–B3; 6 B–K3, B–N5ch; 7 N–B3, BxNch; 8 PxB, Q–K2; 9 Q–B3, N–R3; 10 B–Q3, N–B4; 11 B–QB2, Castles; 12 N–K2, R–K1; 13 N–N3. White's strong pawn centre and two Bishops should outweigh the weakness of his doubled and isolated Queen Bishop Pawns.

A more conservative line is 4 B–B4, N–QB3; 5 N–KB3, B–N5ch; 6 QN–Q2, Q–K2; 7 P–QR3, KNxP!; 8 NxN!, NxN; 9 P–K3, BxNch; 10 QxB, Castles. White's two Bishops give him a slight but perceptible advantage.

DUTCH DEFENCE

1   P–Q4   P–KB4

DIAGRAM 95
(*White to move*)
**White gains the advantage by quiet
positional play**

The gambit 2 P–K4 can be dangerous for inexperienced
players. However, after 2 ... PxP; 3 N–QB3, N–KB3; 4 B–
KN5, N–B3!; 5 P–Q5, N–K4; 6 Q–Q4, N–B2; 7 BxN, KPxB;
8 NxP, P–KB4!; 9 N–N3, P–KN3!; 10 P–KR4, B–R3! Black has
returned the Pawn to obtain a comfortable position.

2   P–KN3   N–KB3
3   B–N2   P–K3

Now White can develop his King Knight to King Rook 3
or King Bishop 3. Both lines are good, for example:

4 N–KR3, P–Q3; 5 Castles, B–K2; 6 P–QB4, Castles; 7 N–B3,
Q–K1!; 8 N–B4, B–Q1; 9 P–K4, P–K4; 10 QPxP, QPxP; 11
N–Q3, PxP; 12 QNxP, N–B3; 13 R–K1. White has the initiative:
his pieces are powerfully posted. Black has an isolated King
Pawn and his development is awkward.

The alternative Knight move might lead to the following
line of play: 4 N–KB3, B–K2; 5 Castles, Castles; 6 P–B4, P–Q4;
7 P–N3, P–B3; 8 N–B3, Q–K1; 9 Q–B2, Q–R4; 10 N–K5, QN–
Q2; 11 N–Q3!; P–KN4; 12 P–B3! and White is ready for the all-
important central advance P–K4. Again White has a strong
initiative.

PART III

How to Win Quickly
in the Openings

HOW TO WIN QUICKLY IN THE OPENING

The object of this section is twofold. It shows you what moves in the opening lead to early loss, and thus enables you to avoid these weak moves.

At the same time you see the consequences of these weak moves. Therefore, if your opponents play these weak moves, you know just how to take advantage of them.

Aside from the practical value of these pitfalls, you will enjoy playing them over. How they are created and how they are exploited makes a drama rich in excitement and thrills. In addition, the key moves of these traps are often beautiful sacrifices that are attractive as well as effective. To succumb to one of these pitfalls is a saddening experience, but to play them over is a lot of fun.

7. OPENING TRAPS

ALEKHINE'S DEFENCE

1	P–K4	N–KB3
2	P–K5	N–Q4
3	P–QB4	N–N3
4	P–Q4	N–B3??

DIAGRAM 96

Black's move (instead of the normal 4 . . . P–Q3) is a blunder that costs a piece.

5	P–Q5!	N–N5

If 5 . . . N–N1; 6 P–B5 and Black loses the unfortunate Knight. And if 5 . . . NxKP; 6 P–B5, N/N3–B5; 7 P–B4 winning a piece.

6	P–B5!	N/N3xP
7	P–QR3	. . .

White wins a piece.

BISHOP'S OPENING

1	P–K4	P–K4
2	B–B4	B–B4
3	Q–R5	N–QB3???

DIAGRAM 97

Black has blundered badly. He saw that his King Pawn was attacked, but he overlooked that White was threatening checkmate!

4   QxBP mate

This is called the " Scholar's Mate." This term is doubtless used sarcastically, and the term " Tyro's Mate " would probably be more appropriate. It is probably seen more often than any other trap in the openings.

BUDAPEST DEFENCE

1	P–Q4	N–KB3
2	P–QB4	P–K4
3	PxP	N–N5
4	B–B4	B–N5ch
5	N–Q2	N–QB3
6	KN–B3	Q–K2
7	P–QR3	KNxKP!

DIAGRAM 98

White can maintain the better development by simply playing
8 NxN, NxN; 9 P–K3. Instead he falls into a curious pitfall.

        8   PxB???   . . .

White has failed to see any purpose behind Black's move,
apparently dismissing it as sheer blunder.

        8 . . .   N–Q6 mate

Smothered mate!

CARO-KANN DEFENCE

1	P–K4	P–QB3
2	P–Q4	P–Q4
3	B–Q3	N–B3?*
4	P–K5!	KN–Q2
5	P–K6!	. . .

DIAGRAM 99

Black does not realize the full extent of his troubles. His
best move is 5 . . . N–B3.

        5 . . .   PxP???

*3 . . . PxP; 4 BxP, N–B3 gives Black a good game.

This leads to a forced mate.

6	Q–R5ch	P–KN3
7	QxNPch!	PxQ
8	BxP mate	

CARO-KANN DEFENCE

1	P–K4	P–QB3
2	P–Q4	P–Q4
3	N–QB3	PxP
4	NxP	N–B3
5	Q–Q3	P–K4?
6	PxP	Q–R4ch
7	B–Q2!	QxKP
8	Castles!	...

DIAGRAM 100

Black has opened up the game prematurely. If now 8 ...
QxN?; 9 R–K1 and White wins the Queen.

8	...	NxN?

Avoiding one trap, Black falls into a different one.

9	Q–Q8ch!!	KxQ
10	B–N5 dbl ch	...

If 10 ... K–K1; 11 R–Q8 mate. And if 10 ... K–B2; 11
B–Q8 mate.

CARO-KANN DEFENCE

1	P–K4	P–QB3
2	P–Q4	P–Q4
3	N–QB3	PxP
4	NxP	B–B4
5	N–N3	B–N3

6	P–KR4	P–KR3
7	N–KB3	P–K3?
8	N–K5!	B–R2
9	B–QB4	N–Q2
10	Q–K2	KN–B3??

DIAGRAM 101

Black's careless **7 ... P–K3** (instead of **7 ... N–Q2!**) has led to trouble. His 10th move is a disastrous blunder.

11	NxKBP!	B–N5ch

If 11 ... KxN; 12 QxPch, K–N3; 13 P–R5 mate—very pretty.

12	P–QB3	Resigns

Black's coming loss of material makes his game hopeless.

CENTRE COUNTER GAME

1	P–K4	P–Q4
2	PxP	QxP
3	N–QB3	Q–QR4
4	P–Q4	N–KB3
5	B–QB4	B–B4
6	B–Q2	P–K3??

DIAGRAM 102

White's last move was sufficiently menacing to put Black on his guard. (6 ... P–B3! was the right move).

	7 N–Q5!	Q–R5

The discovered attack on Black's Queen leaves him only one move.

	8 B–N5ch!	QxB
	9 NxPch	. . .

And White wins the Queen.

CENTRE COUNTER GAME

1	P–K4	P–Q4
2	PxP	QxP
3	N–QB3	Q–QR4
4	P–Q4	N–KB3
5	N–B3	B–N5
6	B–K2	N–B3
7	B–K3	Castles

DIAGRAM 103

Black apparently has a strong initiative: 8 ... P–K4 is a bothersome threat. But White plays with great sublety.

8	N–Q2!	BxB
9	QxB!	NxP?
10	BxN	RxB
11	N–N3	. . .

The point! White wins the Exchange as a result of his trap.

CENTRE GAME

1	P–K4	P–K4
2	P–Q4?	PxP
3	QxP	N–QB3
4	Q–K3	N–B3

5	B–B4	N–K4
6	B–N3	B–N5ch!
7	P–QB3	B–B4!*
8	Q–N3??	. . .

DIAGRAM 104

White has played a time-wasting opening and is now far behind in development. Black's punishment is very drastic!

8	. . .	BxPch!

Winning White's Queen: 9 KxB, NxPch or 9 QxB, N–Q6ch.

DANISH GAMBIT

1	P–K4	P–K4
2	P–Q4	PxP
3	P–QB3	PxP
4	B–QB4	PxP
5	BxP	P–Q4!
6	BxQP	B–N5ch
7	K–B1	N–KB3!
8	Q–R4ch	N–B3
9	BxNch?	PxB

DIAGRAM 105

*If now 8 QxB?, N–Q6ch winning the Queen. White avoids this, but falls into something just as bad.

To all intents and purposes Black has blundered away a piece. Instead of studying the situation carefully, White grabs . . .

10	QxB??	Q–Q8ch
11	Q–K1	B–R3ch
12	N–K2	BxNch
13	K–N1	QxQ mate

White was unfaithful to the spirit of this brilliant gambit!

EVANS GAMBIT

1	P–K4	P–K4
2	N–KB3	N–QB3
3	B–B4	B–B4
4	P–QN4	NxP
5	NxP?	. . .

DIAGRAM 106

White's last is a greedy move that can be refuted by 5 . . . B–Q5 or:

| 5 | . . . | Q–B3! |

Threatens 6 . . . QxP mate and attacks the White Knight as well.

| 6 | P–Q4 | BxP! |
| 7 | QxB | NxBPch |

This Knight fork wins White's Queen. White was too greedy.

FALKBEER COUNTER GAMBIT

1	P–K4	P–K4
2	P–KB4	P–Q4
3	N–KB3	QPxP
4	NxP	N–QB3
5	B–N5	N–B3!
6	NxN	PxN
7	BxPch	B–Q2

DIAGRAM 107

Black has set a neat trap with his strange-looking 5th move. Looking like a complete oversight, this move deludes White into snatching at the win of the Exchange. This proves to be a sad lack of caution on White's part.

　　　　8 BxR??　　　　　　　B–KN5!

Black has trapped White's Queen.

FRENCH DEFENCE

1	P–K4	P–K3
2	P–Q4	P–Q4
3	N–QB3	PxP
4	NxP	N–Q2
5	N–KB3	KN–B3
6	NxNch	NxN
7	B–Q3	B–K2
8	Q–K2	Castles
9	B–KN5	P–QN3?

DIAGRAM 108

Black takes White's 8th move for a mere developing move. It is that, and something more. In fact, the Queen move was the beginning of a trap.

| 10 | BxN! | BxB |
| 11 | Q–K4! | ... |

With this double attack White wins a Rook because of his threat of Q–R7 mate. Black missed the bus!

FRENCH DEFENCE

1	P–K4	P–K3
2	P–Q4	P–Q4
3	N–QB3	B–N5
4	P–K5	P–QB4
5	P–QR3	PxP
6	QxP	N–QB3
7	Q–N4	BxNch
8	PxB	NxP?
9	QxNP	Q–B3
10	B–KR6!!	...

DIAGRAM 109

This ingenious move wins at least the Exchange. Thus, if 10 ... QxB; 11 QxR. Or if 10 ... K–K2; 11 B–KN5 wins Black's Queen. And 10 ... QxQ; 11 BxQ loses for Black.

More complicated is 10 ... N–Q2; 11 B–QN5! threatening 12 Q–B8 mate. Black is unable to save the game.

FRENCH DEFENCE

1	P–K4	P–K3
2	P–Q4	P–Q4
3	N–QB3	N–KB3
4	P–K5	KN–Q2
5	N–B3	P–QB4
6	PxP	BxP
7	B–KB4	N–QB3
8	B–Q3	Q–N3
9	Castles	QxP??

DIAGRAM 110

10 N–QN5! . . .

Threatening the Knight fork 11 N–B7ch and also playing to trap Black's Queen.

10 . . . K–Q1
11 B–Q2 . P–Q5

White was threatening to win the Queen with 12 B–B3.

12 Q–K2 . . .

Now 13 KR–N1 will win Black's Queen.

GIUOCO PIANO

1	P–K4	P–K4
2	N–KB3	N–QB3
3	B–B4	B–B4
4	P–Q3	N–B3
5	N–B3	P–Q3
6	B–KN5	P–KR3
7	BxN	QxB
8	N–Q5	Q–Q1
9	P–B3	. . .

DIAGRAM 111

9	...	B–K3?
10	P–Q4!	PxP

Black must lose a piece: If 10 ... BxN; 11 PxB, N–R4
12 PxB, NxB; 13 Q–R4ch, etc.

11	PxP	B–N3
12	NxB	RPxN
13	P–Q5	N–R4
14	B–Q3!	...

White wins a piece as he threatens P–QN in addition to PxB

GIUOCO PIANO

1	P–K4	P–K4
2	N–KB3	N–QB3
3	B–B4	B–B4
4	P–Q3	N–B3
5	N–B3	Castles
6	B–KN5	P–KR3
7	P–KR4!?	...

DIAGRAM 112

7	...	PxB?
8	PxP	N–KN5
9	P–N6!	NxP
10	NxP!!	NxQ

White was threatening 11 R–R8ch! and 12 Q–R5ch. Despite
the loss of his Queen, White now forces mate by 11 PxPch, RxP
12 BxRch, K–B1; 13 R–R8ch, K–K2; 14 N–Q5ch, K–Q3
15 N–QB4 mate.

GRUENFELD DEFENCE

1	P–Q4	N–KB3
2	P–QB4	P–KN3

3	N–QB3	P–Q4
4	N–B3	B–N2
5	PxP	NxP
6	P–KN3	Castles
7	B–N2	P–QB4
8	Castles	NxN
9	PxN	N–B3

DIAGRAM 113

White's centre is under strong attack.

10	P–K3	Q–R4
11	Q–N3	R–N1
12	B–Q2	B–N5
13	QR–Q1?	. . .

A mistake, directed against Black's threat of 13 ... BxN; 14 BxB, PxP; 15 KPxP, NxP! (*see diagram*).

13	...	PxP!
14	BPxP	Q–R4!

Black's pin wins the Exchange.

HUNGARIAN DEFENCE

1	P–K4	P–K4
2	N–KB3	N–QB3
3	B–B4	B–K2
4	P–Q4	PxP
5	NxP	N–B3
6	N–QB3	P–Q3
7	Castles	Castles
8	P–KR3	R–K1?
9	R–K1	N–Q2??

With his last two moves Black has stripped his position of proper defensive resources. The punishment is swift.

DIAGRAM 114

| 10 | BxPch!! | KxB |

Else he loses the Exchange.

| 11 | N–K6!! | KxN |

The only move to save the Queen.

| 12 | Q–Q5ch | K–B3 |
| 13 | Q–KB5 mate | |

KING'S GAMBIT DECLINED

| 1 | P–K4 | P–K4 |
| 2 | P–KB4 | B–B4 |

DIAGRAM 115

Quite unconcerned about his King Pawn, Black has quietly developed his King Bishop.

| 3 | PxP??? | . . . |

White thoughtlessly snatches the bait.

| 3 | . . . | Q–R5ch! |

Now White sees—too late!—how badly he has exposed his King (4 K–K2, QxKP mate!).

| 4 | P–KN3 | QxKPch |

Black wins a Rook.

KING'S GAMBIT DECLINED

1	P–K4	P–K4
2	P–KB4	B–B4
3	N–KB3	P–Q3
4	B–B4	N–QB3
5	P–B3	B–KN5
6	Q–N3?	BxN
7	PxB	Q–R5ch
8	K–Q1	Q–R4
9	QxP??	...

DIAGRAM 116

White must now be mated or lose his Queen.

9	...	QxBPch

So that if 10 K–K1, B–B7ch!; 11 K–B1, B–N6 dis ch!; 12 K–N1, Q–B7 mate.

10	K–B2	QxKPch

If now 11 K–N3, N–Q5ch wins the Queen.

11	P–Q3	N–Q5ch

Black wins the Queen.

KING'S INDIAN DEFENCE

1	P–Q4	N–KB3
2	P–QB4	P–KN3
3	N–QB3	B–N2
4	P–K4	P–Q3
5	N–B3	Castles
6	B–Q3	B–N5
7	P–KR3	BxN
8	QxB	N–B3
9	B–K3	N–Q2
10	N–K2?	...

DIAGRAM 117

The awkward position of White's pieces allows an amazing reply.

| 10 | ... | N/Q2–K4!! |
| 11 | PxN | NxP |

White's King Bishop is lost!

| 12 | Q–N3 | NxBch |
| 13 | K–Q2 | NxNP |

Black is two Pawns ahead.

MAX LANGE ATTACK

1	P–K4	P–K4
2	N–KB3	N–QB3
3	B–B4	N–B3
4	P–Q4	PxP
5	Castles	B–B4
6	P–K5	P–Q4
7	PxN	PxB
8	R–K1ch	B–K3
9	N–N5	...

DIAGRAM 118

White is threatening to win a piece by 10 NxB, PxN; 11 Q–R5ch.
Black should defend with 9 . . . Q–Q4.

9	. . .	QxP?
10	NxB	PxN
11	Q–R5ch	Q–B2
12	QxB	. . .

White has won a piece.

NIMZOINDIAN DEFENCE

1	P–Q4	N–KB3
2	P–QB4	P–K3
3	N–QB3	B–N5
4	Q–N3	P–B4
5	PxP	N–B3
6	N–B3	N–K5
7	B–Q2	NxQBP
8	Q–B2	Castles
9	P–K4	Q–B3

White's next move is very risky.

10	Castles?	P–QN3
11	B–Q3	P–QR4!
12	P–QR3?	P–R5!
13	PxB??	. . .

DIAGRAM 119

13	. . .	NxNP
14	Q–N1	N–N6 mate

PETROFF'S DEFENCE

1	P–K4	P–K4
2	N–KB3	N–KB3

| 3 | NxP | NxP??* |
| 4 | Q–K2! | ... |

DIAGRAM 120

If now 4 ... N–KB3??; 5 N–B6 dis ch wins Black's Queen.

4	...	Q–K2
5	QxN	P–Q3
6	P–Q4	P–KB3

White has a winning game with 7 P–KB4, N–Q2; 8 N–QB3!, QPxN; 9 N–Q5!

PETROFF'S DEFENCE

1	P–K4	P–K4
2	N–KB3	N–KB3
3	NxP	P–Q3
4	N–KB3	NxP
5	P–Q4	P–Q4
6	B–Q3	N–QB3
7	Castles	B–K2
8	R–K1	B–KN5
9	P–B4	...

DIAGRAM 121

* The safe way is 3 ... P–Q3; 4 N–KB3, NxP; 5 Q–K2, Q–K2.

| 9 | ... | NxQP? |
| 10 | BxN | PxB |

Or 10 . . . NxNch; 11 BxN and White is a piece to the good.

| 10 | QxN | PxN |

He also loses a piece by 11 . . . QxQ; 12 NxQ or 11 . . . BxN;
12 QxQch, RxQ; 13 PxB.

| 12 | QxB | . . . |

White has won a piece.

PHILIDOR'S DEFENCE

1	P–K4	P–K4
2	N–KB3	P–Q3
3	P–Q4	N–Q2
4	B–QB4	KN–B3?

DIAGRAM 122

| 5 | PxP! | QNxP |

Or 5 . . . PxP??; 6 N–N5 and Black cannot defend his King
Bishop Pawn. And after 5 . . . KNxP?; 6 Q–Q5 wins a piece.

6	NxN	PxN
7	BxPch!	KxB!?
8	QxQ	B–QN5ch
9	Q–Q2	. . .

White remains a Pawn ahead.

PHILIDOR'S DEFENCE

1	P–K4	P–K4
2	N–KB3	P–Q3
3	P–Q4	N–Q2
4	B–QB4	B–K2?

DIAGRAM 123

(Black's best is 4 . . . P–QB3!)

5	PxP	PxP?

Or 5 . . . NxP; 6 NxN, PxN; 7 Q–R5 winning material.

6	Q–Q5!	N–N3
7	QxBPch	K–Q2
8	NxPch	K–Q3

White can win in several ways—for example with 9 B–B4.

QUEEN'S FIANCHETTO DEFENCE

1	P–Q4	P–QN3?
2	P–K4	B–N2
3	B–Q3	P–KB4??
4	PxP	BxP?

DIAGRAM 124

Black wins a Rook—but loses his King.

5	Q–R5ch	P–N3
6	PxP	N–KB3
7	PxP dis ch!!	. . .

A neat point completely overlooked by Black.

7	. . .	NxQ
8	B–N6 mate	

Well-deserved punishment for Black!

QUEEN'S GAMBIT ACCEPTED

1	P–Q4	P–Q4
2	P–QB4	PxP
3	P–K3	P–QN4?
4	P–QR4	P–QB3
5	PxP	PxP??
6	Q–B3!	. . .

DIAGRAM 125

Black's whole opening is wrong; his last move is a blunder that costs a piece.

No matter how Black plays, he must lose a piece. The moral of this very important trap is that Black must be circumspect in his efforts to hold on to the gambit Pawn. On move 4, by the way, 4 . . . P–QR3 is met by 5 PxP and Black cannot retake.

QUEEN'S GAMBIT ACCEPTED

1	P–Q4	P–Q4
2	P–QB4	PxP
3	N–KB3	B–N5
4	P–K3	P–K3
5	BxP	N–KB3
6	N–B3	N–B3
7	Castles	B–Q3
8	B–K2	Castles
9	P–K4?	. . .

DIAGRAM 126

White has the praiseworthy idea of opening a diagonal for his
Queen Bishop; he overlooks however, that this gives Black a
chance to win material.

9	...	BxN!
10	BxB	NxQP!
11	QxN???	BxPch

Followed by 12 ... QxQ winning White's Queen.

QUEEN'S GAMBIT DECLINED

1	P–Q4	P–Q4
2	P–QB4	P–K3
3	N–QB3	N–KB3
4	B–N5	QN–Q2
5	PxP	PxP

DIAGRAM 127

In view of the pin on Black's King Knight, White believes
he can win a Pawn. Normally he would be quite justified; but
here he is all wrong!

6	NxP??	NxN!!
7	BxQ	B–N5ch
8	Q–Q2	BxQch
9	KxQ	KxB

Black has won a piece.

QUEEN'S GAMBIT DECLINED

1	P-Q4	P-Q4
2	P-QB4	P-K3
3	N-QB3	N-KB3
4	B-N5	QN-Q2
5	P-K3	B-K2
6	N-B3	Castles
7	R-B1	P-B3
8	Q-B2	P-QR3
9	PxP	KPxP
10	B-Q3	R-K1
11	Castles	P-R3
12	B-KB4	N-R4?

DIAGRAM 128

13	NxP!	PxN??

After 13 . . . NxB; 14 NxN Black has lost only a Pawn.

14	B-B7	. . .

White wins the Queen.

QUEEN'S GAMBIT DECLINED

1	P-Q4	P-Q4
2	P-QB4	P-K3
3	N-QB3	N-KB3
4	B-N5	QN-Q2
5	P-K3	P-B3
6	N-B3	Q-R4
7	N-Q2	B-N5
8	Q-B2	Castles
9	B-Q3?	. . .

DIAGRAM 129

White's last move looks like perfectly good development, but 9 B–K2 is much better.

	9 . . .		PxP!
	10 BxN		BPxB!

The only move to win a piece.

| | 11 QxP | | NxB |

QUEEN'S GAMBIT DECLINED

1	P–Q4	P–Q4
2	P–QB4	P–QB3
3	N–KB3	N–B3
4	P–K3	P–K3
5	N–B3	QN–Q2
6	B–Q3	B–Q3
7	Castles	Castles
8	P–K4	PxKP
9	NxP	NxN
10	BxN	P–K4?

DIAGRAM 130

Black wants to free his game, but he has overlooked an important tactical trick.

| | 11 PxP | | NxP |

12	NxN	BxN
13	BxPch!	KxB
14	Q–R5ch	K–N1
15	QxB	. . .

White has won a Pawn.

QUEEN'S INDIAN DEFENCE

1	P–Q4	N–KB3
2	P–QB4	P–K3
3	N–KB3	P–QN3
4	P–KN3	B–N2
5	B–N2	B–K2
6	Castles	Castles
7	N–B3	N–K5
8	B–Q2	NxN
9	N–N5?	. . .

DIAGRAM 131

Apparently Black is in trouble: he is threatened with mate and he is also in danger on the long diagonal.

9	. . .	NxPch!

If now 10 QxN, BxB wins a piece for Black!

10	K–R1	BxBch
11	KxB	BxN

Black has won a piece.

QUEEN'S INDIAN DEFENCE

1	P–Q4	N–KB3
2	P–QB4	P–K3
3	N–KB3	P–QN3
4	B–N5	B–N2
5	P–K3	P–KR3!
6	B–R4	B–N5ch

DIAGRAM 132

7 QN–Q2?	P–KN4!
8 B–N3	P–N5!

If White's King Knight moves, then 9 . . . N–K5 wins a piece
for Black.

9 P–QR3	PxN!
10 PxB	PxP
11 BxNP	BxP

Black has won a piece, thanks to White's weak 7th move.

QUEEN'S PAWN OPENING

1	P–Q4	P–Q4
2	N–KB3	P–QB4
3	B–B4	N–QB3
4	P–K3	N–B3
5	N–B3	B–N5
6	B–QN5	P–K3
7	P–KR3	B–R4
8	P–KN4	B–N3
9	N–K5	R–B1?

DIAGRAM 133

Black's last move is a mistake that costs the Exchange
(9 . . . Q–N3 was the right move).

10	NxN	PxN
11	B-QR6	R-R1
12	B-N7	...

The White Bishops co-operate admirably to force the win of the Exchange. Black's badgered Rook has no refuge.

RETI OPENING

1	N-KB3	P-Q4
2	P-B4	PxP
3	N-R3	P-K4
4	NxKP	BxN
5	Q-R4ch	P-QN4!
6	QxB	B-N2
7	P-QN3	Q-Q3!
8	B-N2?	P-B6!!

DIAGRAM 134

Black's last move is a very ingenious stroke that wins a piece by force.

Thus, if 9 PxP, QxN wins the Knight.

Again, if 9 QxQ, PxQ and Black attacks two pieces, of which one must be lost.

Finally, if 9 BxP??, QxQ wins White's Queen out of hand.

Thus it turns out that White's 8th move was a serious blunder.

RUY LOPEZ

1	P-K4	P-K4
2	N-KB3	N-QB3
3	B-N5	P-QR3
4	B-R4	N-B3
5	N-B3	P-Q3
6	P-Q4	P-QN4

DIAGRAM 135

White's safest course is **7 PxP.**

7	B–N3?	NxQP!
8	NxN	PxN
9	QxP?	. . .

Naturally White does not want to lose a Pawn—but now he loses a piece.

9	. . .	P–B4

And after White's Queen retreats, **10 . . . P–B5** traps the White Bishop.

RUY LOPEZ

1	P–K4	P–K4
2	N–KB3	N–QB3
3	B–N5	P–QR3
4	B–R4	N–B3
5	Castles	NxP
6	P–Q4	P–QN4
7	B–N3	P–Q4
8	PxP	B–K3
9	P–B3	B–K2

White's next move prepares the trap.

10	R–K1	Castles
11	N–Q4	Q–Q2?

DIAGRAM 136

Black falls into the trap.

| | 12 | NxB | . . . |

This move wins a piece, for if 12 . . . QxN or 12 . . . PxN;
13 RxN! and Black's Queen Pawn is pinned.

RUY LOPEZ

1	P–K4	P–K4
2	N–KB3	N–QB3
3	B–N5	P–QR3
4	B–R4	P–Q3
5	BxNch	PxB
6	P–Q4	P–B3
7	N–B3	R–N1
8	Q–Q3	N–K2
9	B–K3!	. . .

DIAGRAM 137

Black grabs the unprotected Pawn:

9	. . .	RxP
10	PxP	BPxP
11	NxP!	PxN?
12	QxQch	RxQ
13	Castles (Q) ch!	. . .

White comes out the Exchange ahead. Note that if 10 . . .
QPxP??; 11 QxQch, KxQ; 12 Castles(Q)ch winning a whole
Rook.

RUY LOPEZ

1	P–K4	P–K4
2	N–KB3	N–QB3
3	B–N5	P–QR3
4	B–R4	N–B3
5	N–B3	B–B4
6	NxP	NxN

7	P–Q4	B–N5
8	PxN	NxP
9	. . .	NxN
10	PxN	B–R4?

10 . . . B–K2 is correct.

11	B–R3!	P–QN3

DIAGRAM 138

12	P–K6!	Q–B3

White threatened 13 P–K7! or 13 QxKNP.

13	BxPch	K–Q1
14	B–B6 dis ch!	QxQ
15	P–K7 mate	

SCOTCH GAMBIT

1	P–K4	P–K4
2	N–KB3	N–QB3
3	P–Q4	PxP
4	B–QB4	B–QB4
5	N–N5	N–R3
6	Q–R5	N–K4

DIAGRAM 139

Black's last move is a mistake (6 . . . Q–K2 is the right way).

7	N–K6!!	QPxN

White wins a piece no matter how Black plays.

| | 8 QxN/K5 | ... |

It is impossible for Black to defend himself against the threats of 9 QxB or 9 QxNP or 9 BxN.

SICILIAN DEFENCE

1	P–K4	P–QB4
2	N–KB3	P–K3
3	P–Q4	PxP
4	NxP	N–KB3
5	N–QB3	B–N5
6	P–K5	N–Q4
7	Q–N4	P–KN3
8	P–QR3	Q–R4?

DIAGRAM 140

Black relies on a pin which turns out to be valueless.

| 9 | PxB! | QxR |

If Black does not capture, he is a piece down.

| 10 | N–N3 | ... |

The Black Queen is trapped; every possible square available to her is covered by a White piece.

SICILIAN DEFENCE

1	P–K4	P–QB4
2	N–KB3	P–Q3
3	P–Q4	PxP
4	NxP	N–KB3
5	N–QB3	N–B3
6	B–K2	P–KN3
7	B–K3	B–N2
8	Castles	N–KN5?
9	BxN!	...

DIAGRAM 141

Black must lose a piece, for example 9 . . . NxN; 10 BxB; or
9 . . . BxN; 10 B/N4xB, BxN; 11 BxNP.

	9	. . .	BxB
	10	NxN!	. . .

White is now certain of winning a piece, for example 10 . . .
PxN; 11 QxB or 10 . . . BxQ; 11 NxQ. This complicated trap
is well worth knowing.

SICILIAN DEFENCE

1	P–K4	P–QB4
2	N–QB3	N–QB3
3	P–KN3	P–K3
4	B–N2	N–B3
5	KN–K2	P–Q4
6	PxP	PxP
7	P–Q4	B–N5
8	PxP	BxP
9	NxP?	N–Q5

White must try 10 N/Q5–B3.

10	NxNch?	. . .

DIAGRAM 142

10 ...	QxN

Note this: if 11 B–B1, N–B6 mate!

11	P–KB3	QxP!!
12	BxQ	NxBch
13	K–B1	B–KR6 mate

THREE KNIGHTS' GAME

1	P–K4	P–K4
2	N–KB3	N–QB3
3	N–B3	B–N5
4	B–N5	KN–K2
5	Castles	Castles
6	P–Q4	PxP
7	NxP	P–Q4?
8	PxP	BxN
9	PxB	QxP

DIAGRAM 143

10	NxN!	PxN

Or 10 ... QxQ; 11 NxQch and White will be two pieces ahead. If 10 ... QxB; 11 NxNch winning a piece.

11	QxQ	PxQ

He also loses the Exchange after 11 ... NxQ; 12 BxP, B–K3; 13 BxR.

12	B–R3	...

White wins the Exchange.

TWO KNIGHTS' GAME

1	P–K4	P–K4
2	N–KB3	N–QB3
3	B–B4	N–B3
4	N–N5	P–Q4

5	PxP	NxP
6	P–Q4!	PxP?
7	Castles	B–K3
8	R–K1	B–K2

DIAGRAM 144

White has a surprise sacrifice.

9	RxB!	PxR
10	NxKP	Q–Q2
11	BxN	. . .

Now Black cannot play 11 . . . QxB??? because of 12 NxBPch winning the Queen. White therefore retains Bishop and Knight for a Rook—a material advantage for White.

VIENNA GAME

1	P–K4	P–K4
2	N–QB3	N–KB3
3	P–B4	P–Q4
4	BPxP	NxP
5	P–Q3!?	Q–R5ch?
6	P–KN3	NxP

DIAGRAM 145

Black *appears* to have a very strong game.

7	N–B3!		Q–R4
8	NxP		K–Q1

Also bad is 8 . . . NxR; 9 NxPch, K–Q1; 10 NxR, B–KN5; 11 B–N2 winning a piece.

9	N–B4!		Q–N5

Or 9 . . . Q–R3; 10 N–K2! and wins.

10	B–R3		. . .

White wins the Queen.

PART IV

The Middle Game

THE MIDDLE GAME

A famous atomic scientist has said that every scientific invention consists of a number of ideas which are ridiculous as a combination; yet if some original idea is added to them and they are somewhat rearranged, they yield a brilliantly effective device.

So it is with chess combinations. The moves at first seem absurd, but there is a ruling idea behind them which makes them purposeful and hence meaningful.

In almost every combination in this section the mechanics are astounding at first glance. This element of surprise will delight you, but remember that there is profound logic behind it. Master the meaning behind each combinative idea and you will be well on the way to chess mastery.

8. ATTACKING MOTIFS

PINNING ATTACKS

DIAGRAM 146
(*Black to move*)

Black's Queen and Bishop aim at White's King Knight Pawn. Black has the initiative, to be sure, but White seems to have his weaknesses well covered. A fearsome pin teaches White a saddening lesson:

| | 1 . . . | QxPch! |
| | 2 QxQ | RxR |

All that is left for White is to play 3 QxB, which leaves him the Exchange and two Pawns down—an easy win for Black.

129

DIAGRAM 147
(*White to move*)

White can win a Pawn by moving his pinned Knight, thus
1 NxQ, RxRch; 2 KxR, BxQ; 3 NxP. However, White has a
much stronger move in the killing pin:

	1 B–QR3!!	RxRch

If 1 . . . QxB; 2 QxP mate.

	2 RxR	BxN
	3 BxQch	RxB
	4 QxB	. . .

White's enormous material advantage is decisive.

DIAGRAM 148
(*Black to move*)

White's Queen, which is on the same diagonal with his King
is tied down to its present square to prevent . . . QxNP mate
Therefore:

	1 . . .	B–N4!

If 2 QxB, QxNP mate.

	2 P–B4	BxP!

The pin wins White's Queen, for if 3 QxB, QxNP mate. Black
took ruthless advantage of White's helplessness.

DIAGRAM 149
(*White to move*)

White moves his attacked Queen by attacking Black's pinned Knight a second time:

      1 Q–B4   N–K3

Counter attack is the only defence. But White saves his Queen with:

      2 Q–QR4ch   Q–B3

Else White plays BxQ.

      3 B–QN5   . . .

Pinning and winning Black's Queen.

DIAGRAM 150
(*Black to move*)

White has the pin, but Black has the win!

      1 . . .   RxB!
      2 RxR   Q–QN2

To this pin there is only one reply.

      3 Q–KN2   Q–N8ch!
      4 Q–N1   Q–K5ch!
      5 Q–N2   QxQch
      6 KxQ   N–B5ch

Followed by 7 . . . NxR and wins.

DIAGRAM 151
(*White to move*)

The pin on Black's Knight is disastrous for him because the Knight *cannot be guarded by a Pawn*. Worse yet, Black's Kingside has been weakened by the Pawn advances.

1	R–K6!!	PxR

Else Black loses his Knight.

2	QxPch	K–R1
3	BxNch	any
4	Q–R7 mate	

DIAGRAM 152
(*White to move*)

Pins can be very dangerous, but they don't always work. In this position it is pointless for White to play NxQ because of . . . RxQ. In other words, White's Knight is pinned. What's more, Black threatens mate by . . . Q–Q8ch, etc.

1	R–N8ch!	KxR

1 . . . RxR allows 2 NxQ (no pin!).

2	NxR dbl ch	. . .

By giving check, White wins the Queen.

DIAGRAM 153
(*White to move*)

White is the Exchange down, and should lose the game on material disadvantage.

However, he has an interesting resource that wins the game for him:

1 P–K8/Qch!   KxQ

Forced, of course.

2 B–R4!   . . .

Pinned and winning the helpless Rook, which cannot be defended!

DIAGRAM 154
(*Black to move*)

White builds up decisive pressure with a forceful pin:

1 . . .   BxBch
2 NxB   Q–N3!
3 QxP   NxP!

Discovered attack on the White Queen. If now 4 Q–K5, R–K3 drives her off.

4 Q–Q7   N–Q3!

White's pinned Knight is lost.

KNIGHT FORKS

DIAGRAM 155
(*Black to move*)

Here too it takes imagination to see the winning combination, for who would dream of giving up his Queen for a mere Knight?

	1 ...	QxN!
	2 QxQ	N–K6ch
	3 K moves	NxQ

Black's Queen sacrifice has resulted in the win of a clear piece. The preliminary pattern for the Knight fork is often seen in practical play.

DIAGRAM 156
(*White to move*)

White is all set for the forking check NxBPch. Unfortunately his Knight is pinned. Therefore:

1 QxR!	BPxQ

White's Knight is unpinned. He is ready for the fork.

	2 N–B7ch	K moves
	3 NxQ	RxN

By means of his (temporary) Queen sacrifice White has won the Exchange.

DIAGRAM 157
(*Black to move*)

Black eyes the forking check ... N–K7ch eagerly, but it doesn't work because White's Bishop is on guard. Therefore:

1	...	QxB!
2	PxQ	N–K7ch
3	K moves	NxQ

Black's combination has won a clear piece for him. His imaginative first move was the key to the whole winning process.

DIAGRAM 158
(*White to move*)

White is the Exchange down, but he has played for this position and now sets the stage for a winning Knight fork.

| 1 | QxRch! | RxQ |
| 2 | N–K6ch | ... |

Now, no matter where Black moves his King, there follows 3 RxQ and White's material advantage is speedily decisive. It takes imagination to see White's first move; the rest follows smoothly enough.

DISCOVERED ATTACKS

DIAGRAM 159
(*Black to move*)

Black's Queen Pawn is pinned; if he moves it, he loses his
Queen. Consequently, his first move comes as a shattering
surprise:

1 ...   P–Q6!

Exposing his Queen to attack, but attacking White's Queen
—and his Queen Bishop, too. If now 2 BxQ, PxQ and *White
must lose a piece*. Verify this.

2 QxP   QxB

Black has won a piece. White had no choice.

DIAGRAM 160
(*White to move*)

White cannot win the game by force, but he can gain a considerable advantage by:

1 RxPch!   ...

Surprisingly, this Rook cannot very well be captured. Thus
if 1 ... PxR; 2 B–N6ch or 1 ... BxR; 2 B–N5ch and in either
case White wins the Queen by a discovered attack.

1 ...   K–B1

Black can never castle now.

DIAGRAM 161
(*White to move*)

Black seems to have a solid position, but this impression is misleading. White has a winning move in the following:

    1 P–Q5!   ...

This move attacks Black's Queen. But that is not all. White's Pawn move uncovers an attack on Black's Knight. If Black could move his Queen to a square from which it could protect the Knight, all would be well. This is impossible; so White wins a piece.

DIAGRAM 162
(*White to move*)

This position looks like a draw. Actually White has a forced win, thanks to a powerful discovered attack on Black's unprotected Queen.

    1 Q–K6ch!   K–R2

Note that 1 ... K–R4 leads to the same result.

    2 N–B6ch!   ...

This check also sets up a discovered attack on Black's Queen. Black must get out of check, and meanwhile he loses his Queen.

DIAGRAM 163
(*Black to move*)

Again it requires imagination to see how Black can set a discovered attack in motion. This much we know: the first move must be forceful.

       1   ...   N–K6!

Attacking White's Rook and Bishop and therefore forcing White's reply.

       2 R–K1   N–B5ch

Giving check and uncovering a discovered attack against White's unprotected Rook. Black wins the Exchange.

DISCOVERED CHECKS

DIAGRAM 164
(*White to move*)

White spies a flaw in Black's seemingly solid position. A discovered check is the key.

       1 RxN!!   PxR
       2 QxRch!!   KxQ
       3 PxP dis ch   ...

White wins back the Queen, regardless of whether Black moves his King or interposes his Queen. The vital point was depriving Black's Rook of protection by his Knight.

DIAGRAM 165
(*Black to move*)

Black forces a decisive material advantage by sacrificing his Queen:

| 1 | ... | QxRch! |
| 2 | KxQ | N–B4 dis ch |

Discovered check with attack on the Queen.

No matter how White replies, he loses his Queen, and is then left with a whole Rook down. Thus Black owes his success to his alert realization that a discovered check can be set up.

DIAGRAM 166
(*White to move*)

White's dynamic sacrifice sets the stage for a discovered check:

| 1 | R–R8ch! | KxR |
| 2 | P–K6 dis ch | ... |

Discovered check plus attack on the Queen — a venomous combination.

| 2 | ... | Q–KN2 |
| 3 | BxQch | ... |

White has an overwhelming advantage material.

DIAGRAM 167
(*White to move*)

Black's badly boxed-in King, unassisted by his other pieces, makes an easy victim. But it takes really piercing imagination to foresee the finish.

1	QxPch!!	KxQ
2	B–R5ch!!	KxR
3	B–B7 mate	

It is a particularly deadly discovered check that forces mate on the move.

DIAGRAM 168
(*White to move*)

Instead of trying to save his attacked Knight, White goes in for double attack:

1	R–K7!	BxN

There is no good alternative.

2	RxPch	K–R1

Now comes a discovered check winning a piece.

3	RxB dis ch	K–N1
4	RxB	. . .

White is a piece ahead.

DIAGRAM 169
(*Black to move*)

Black wins the Exchange by:

1	...	NxP!
2	QxN	QxQch
3	KxQ	P–B6 dis ch

This discovered check wins a White Rook, as White must concentrate on getting his King into safety.

4	NxB	PxR
5	RxRch	KxR!

After 6 BxP, RxB Black wins easily.

DOUBLE ATTACKS

DIAGRAM 170
(*Black to move*)

It takes real imagination to spy out the weaknesses in White's camp, but Black is equal to the task:

1 ...	NxBch!

Very prosaic—but forceful. 2 NxN??? is out of the question, as it loses the Queen. Therefore:

2 QxN	Q–Q5ch!

No matter what White plays, Black continues 3 ... QxN/
QB6, having won a piece. Another example of double attack
with check.

DIAGRAM 171
(*White to move*)

White has a crushing double attack in view, but he needs a
preparatory move before it can operate effectively.

1	BxN!	BxB
2	Q–K4!	...

The double attack White had in mind. He threatens Q–R7
mate and at the same time attacks Black's Queen Rook. Black
can guard against either threat, but not against both. The
result: White wins a Rook.

DIAGRAM 172
(*White to move*)

Though White does not have to sacrifice any material, his
winning method is bright and neat. Many players might overlook
it precisely because it is so simple.

1	NxN!	QxN

Black cannot recapture with his Queen Pawn, which is *pinned*.

2	BxPch	...

The double attack, directed against Black's King and Queen,
White wins Black's Queen.

DIAGRAM 173
(*Black to move*)

White is on the defensive, but everything seems to be well defended for the moment. However, this is an illusion, as Black proves by sacrificing the Exchange:

    1 ...   RxB!

White must recapture, of course; but then he runs into a nasty check.

    2 RxR   BxPch

Black gives check and at the same time attacks White's Rook. Black comes out a piece ahead.

DOUBLE CHECKS

DIAGRAM 174
(*White to move*)

Double checks are a particularly powerful form of double attack. White has a double check on 1 BxB dbl ch, but it leads to nothing. The right way is:

    1 B–Q6 dbl ch!   KxB

Forced, otherwise he loses the Queen.

    2 R–Q3

This pin wins Black's Queen, with a winning material advantage for White.

DIAGRAM 175
(*White to move*)

White wins brilliantly:

    1   Q–B8ch!!!   KxQ

The Queen must be captured. But now comes the double
check that forces the win for White—with a Queen down!

    2   N–N6 dbl ch   K–Q1

(Or 2 . . . K–N1 with the same result). Neither checking piece
can be captured.

    3   R–B8 mate

DIAGRAM 176
(*White to move*)

White has several discovered checks; which is the strongest?
What is puzzling about the choice is that White's own Queen
is under attack.

    1   N–B8 dbl ch!   . . .

Because this is a *double* check, Black cannot capture either
the Knight or the Queen.

    1   . . .   K–Q1
    2   NxQ   . . .

White's enormous material advantage decides.

OVERBURDENED PIECES

DIAGRAM 177
(White to move)

White's threat of Q–N7 mate is parried by Black's posting of his Queen at the King Bishop 1 square. White's problem is, how can he remove the Queen from its valuable square? Here is his solution of the problem:

> 1 R–K8!!   QxR

The pinned Queen is overburdened and has no choice.

> 2 Q–N7 mate

DIAGRAM 178
(White to move)

Material is even, and so (apparently) is the position. Black's Queen is defended by his Rook. White's Queen is attacked but undefended. You might think the Black Queen is the more secure of the two Queens, but . . .

> 1 R–B8ch!   RxR

Black has no choice. His Rook is overburdened.

> 2 QxQ   . . .

White's material advantage wins easily.

DIAGRAM 179
(*Black to move*)

This position seems to lack character. Yet danger often lurks in such harmless-looking positions. Black proves this with an unexpected stroke:

1 ...   N–B4!

Now White's Knight is overburdened. Any move with that piece loses valuable material.

2 NxN   RxBch

White has no time to save his Knight. After he gets out of check, Black wins with ... BxN.

DIAGRAM 180
(*Black to move*)

Black can defend himself against all threats by playing ... Q–N2. But Black does not want to play defensively; instead, he finds an aggressive continuation:

1 ...   B–Q6ch!

Now 2 K–N2??? is out of the question because of 2 ... R–B7 mate (or 2 ... QxN mate).

2 QxB   QxRch

Black wins easily with his material advantage.

DIAGRAM 181
(*White to move*)

White gets nowhere with RxRch, as Black has ... QxR
in reply.

The right way depends on a Queen sacrifice:

      1 Q–K5!!   RxR

Black's Queen was overburdened, no longer able to guard
the Black Rook in the face of the threat of 2 QxNP mate. (If
1 ... QxQ; 2 RxR mate).

      2 QxQ

White's material advantage wins easily.

DIAGRAM 182
(*White to move*)

White is a Pawn ahead. He can try 1 RxRch, QxR; 2 QxQBP,
but then, after 2 ... Q–K7ch the position is very unclear.

Actually, he has a very quick win by overburdening the Black
Queen:

      1 Q–KN4ch!   QxQ

He cannot afford to lose his Queen.

      2 RxRch   K–N2
      3 PxQ and wins

DIAGRAM 183
(*White to move*)

In moving away his attacked Rook, White relies on the theme of the overburdened piece.

           1 R–K8ch!!   RxR

Black's Bishop, being pinned, is overburdened and cannot capture the impertinent Rook. Result: Black will be checkmated.

           2 QxBch   K–R1
           3 QxRch   Q–B1
           4 QxQ mate

REMOVING GUARDING PIECES

DIAGRAM 184
(*Black to move*)

Black is the Exchange ahead and has a threatening attack along the open King Rook file. Luckily, White has his Queen effectively posted to prevent . . . Q–R8 mate. Here Black sees his chance to win by removing the guarding piece:

           1 . . .   R–K6!

If now 2 QxR, Q–R8 mate.

           2 Q–N2   RxP

White is helplessly lost.

DIAGRAM 185
(*White to move*)

Black's Knight is very awkwardly situated—it has no retreat.
Luckily, it is guarded by the Black Bishop. White now saws
off this protection, winning the helpless Knight.

1	B–B8!	BxB

Black has nothing better.

2	RxBch	K–N2
3	KxN	. . .

White's material advantage must win.

DIAGRAM 186
(*White to move*)

White starts with a double attack which forces Black's hand:

1	Q–K6ch	. . .

Double attack with check. Black has only one move to guard
his Knight.

1	. . .	K–N2

But now White drives away the guard.

2	Q–K7ch	. . .

Followed by 3 QxN with an easy win.

DIAGRAM 187
(*Black to move*)

Black's procedure illustrates a dexterous little trick worth knowing. White's Queen is attacked by the Black Queen and guarded by the Knight. Black removes the guard with:

1 ...   BxN

If now 2 PxB??? or 2 RxB???, QxQ and White can resign.

2   QxQ   BxQ

Black wins with a piece to the good.

LAST-RANK COMBINATIONS

DIAGRAM 188
(*Black to move*)

If Black is careless, he can blunder away his chances with 1 ... Q–N8ch; 2 Q–B1, R–Q8??; 3 R–B8ch and White checkmates on the unprotected last rank. Instead, Black forces the win artistically:

1 ...   Q–N7!!

White has no good reply. If 2 QxQ, R–Q8 mate. If 2 Q–K1, QxR!; 3 QxQ, R–Q8ch and mate next move.

2 R–Q3   Q–N8ch

Black wins the Rook.

DIAGRAM 189
(*Black to move*)

At first sight this position looks jumbled. It is not even easy
to see that White is weak on the last rank because he has a
" loophole " for his King to escape. And yet—

1 ...   N–N5!!

Now White's King cannot escape to the King Rook 2 square.
Black threatens 2 ... Q–R7 mate.

2 QxQ   R–B8 mate

Another possibility was 2 PxN, R–B8 mate.

DIAGRAM 190
(*Black to move*)

Black is two Pawns down and will lose a third after his Queen
moves. He seems hopelessly lost, and yet he has an exquisite
resource:

1 ...   R–B4!!!

This brilliant move wins. If 2 RxQ, R–B8 mate. If 2 PxR,
Q–Q8 mate.

        2 RxR   QxQ

With his overwhelming material advantage, Black has an easy win.

DIAGRAM 191
(*Black to move*)

Black's pieces, co-operate beautifully in a mating attack. The key move is:

        1 ...   BxP!!

If now 2 RxB or QxB, Q–B8ch and mate next move.

        2 Q–N3   ...

Parrying the threat of 2 ... QxP mate or 2 ... BxP mate.

        2 ...   Q–B8ch!
        3 RxQ   RxR mate

DIAGRAM 192
(*White to move*)

With Black's Queen shut off from the defence, White has a forceful finish available.

        1 N–B6   B–N2
        2 N–K8!   B–R3

After 2 ... P–K5 White wins in the same way.

        3 Q–B8ch!   BxQ
        4 RxB mate!

White's Queen sacrifice is spectacular indeed. But Black's pieces were miserably posted.

DIAGRAM 193
(*Black to move*)

White has set a neat trap. He hopes for 1 . . . RxQ?; 2 NxRch followed by 3 NxQ, which leaves him with two clear Pawns ahead and an easy win. But Black does not oblige:

1 ...   QxN!

White's last rank is vulnerable!

2 QxR   Q–K8 mate

In making plans for a combination, be sure the last rank is safe from attack!

DIAGRAM 194
(*Black to move*)

It takes a master to see that White has a last-rank weakness.

1 ...   B–KB4!!

If now 2 QxB, NxBch; 3 K–R1, R–B8ch; 4 Q–N1, RxQ mate.

2 NxB   QxN!!
3 QxQ   NxBch
4 K–R1   R–B8ch
5 Q–N1   RxQ mate

DIAGRAM 195
(*White to move*)

White is able to win in interesting fashion thanks to the un-favourable position of the Black King on the last rank.

    1   RxP!!   QxQ

If 1 . . . NxR; 2 Q–B8ch forces mate.

    2   R–K8 mate

Black's weakness on the last rank made it possible for White to offer the Rook and the Queen to force mate.

DIAGRAM 196
(*Black to move*)

Black seems to have a draw at best, yet he finds a subtle winning combination because of a last-rank weakness.

    1   . . .   B–R3!!

If now 2 BxB, Q–B7ch; 3 K–R1, Q–B8ch!; 4 RxQ, RxR mate!

    2   R–K1   BxBch
    3   QxB   R–B8ch!

Black wins the Queen for the Rook.

QUEENING COMBINATIONS

DIAGRAM 197
(*Black to move*)

A queening Pawn is often captured, but may nevertheless bring about a decisive gain of material.

1	...	RxNch!
2	KxR	P–K7
3	R–B1	...

Forced.

3	...	PxR/Qch
4	KxQ	NxB

Black is two pieces ahead.

DIAGRAM 198
(*White to move*)

White is the Exchange ahead and is bound to win. To win quickly, he makes use of his passed Pawn:

1	RxB!	RxR
2	RxR	KxR

If 2 ... QxR; 3 Q–Q8 mate.

3	Q–Q7ch	QxQ
4	PxQ	...

White's passed Pawn cannot be prevented from queening.

DIAGRAM 199
(*Black to move*)

Material is about even and a draw seems to be the likely out-come. Yet Black has a surprising win based on the queening power of a Pawn.

1	...	R–R6ch!
2	K–Q2	RxB!

This leaves Black a piece down, but he knows what he is doing

3	PxR	P–R6!

The Pawn must become a Queen!

DIAGRAM 200
(*White to move*)

A " queening " Pawn doesn't always become a Queen—for example:

1	QxPch!!	PxQ
2	P–N7ch	K–R2
3	PxN/ch!	...

Of course, not 3 PxR/Q???, Q–R6 mate!

3	...	K–R1
4	R–N8 mate	

A very pretty combination.

DIAGRAM 201
(*White to move*)

At first sight it looks as if White must lose his far-advanced,
passed Queen Bishop Pawn. But if he plays his cards right, he
can win:

       1 R–Q8ch!   RxR

White does not recapture here, promoting to a Queen, because
his new Queen would at once be lost.

       2 R–B8ch!   KxR
       3 PxR/Qch   . . .

White's material advantage is overwhelming.

INTERFERENCE COMBINATIONS

DIAGRAM 202
(*White to move*)

White has several winning lines, but the quickest is based
on a glorious Queen sacrifice:

       1 Q–K6!!!   . . .

This cuts off the action of Black's Bishop or his Rook at Queen
Rook 3.

       1 . . .   BxQ
       2 N–B5 dis ch   K–N1
       3 N–K7 mate

If 1 . . . RxQ; 2 N–N6 dis ch, K–N1; 3 R–R8 mate.

DIAGRAM 203
(*White to move*)

This type of combination involves the blocking of a vital
defensive line. Neither 1 Q–N7ch or 1 RxPch wins, but there
is a way to make them work:

	1	B–B7!!	QxB

Or 1 . . . RxB; 2 Q–N7ch!!, RxQ; 3 RxP mate!

	2	RxPch!!	QxR
	3	Q–N7ch	KxP
	4	R–R1 mate	

ZUGZWANG COMBINATIONS

DIAGRAM 204
(*White to move*)

To win, White must keep up the pressure of the pin.

	1	RxR!	RxR
	2	P–KR4!	P–R3
	3	K–N2	P–KN4
	4	P–R5!	. . .

When Black runs out of Pawn moves, he will be in *Zugzwang*
(see next page); he will have to move his King, losing his Rook

DIAGRAM 205
(*White to move*)

Zugzwang is a German word describing a situation on the chessboard where a player loses because it is his turn to move. The word means " move-compulsion."

1   R–B7!

Black is lost.   Sooner or later he will have to move his King or his Knight or his Bishop or his Rook.   Whatever he does, he will lose a piece.

PART V
The Endgame

THE ENDGAME

In chess the endgame is the "payoff." It is that part of the struggle where the ultimate outcome is determined. Proper handling of endings requires accurate calculation, precision, and imagination.

Endings are also deceptive. Often they look simple, even when they harbour tricky possibilities that require the most demanding kind of study. No wonder that all the World Champions have been superlative endgame players.

The endings discussed in the following pages are intended as an invitation to further study of this very important and very rewarding part of chess. Become a better endgame player and you will be a better chess player.

9. BASIC ENDGAMES

KING AND PAWN ENDINGS

This type of ending looks "simple" to the beginner because of the considerably reduced material on the board. In actual play we find that these endings are not so simple, as they are full of finesses.

All these endings revolve about the queening of a Pawn. Diagram 206 shows a basic position.

DIAGRAM 206

If it is Black's move, White wins. If it is White's move, the position is drawn

The fight centres here about White's effort to queen his Pawn. Black's King stands on the queening square. If it is Black's move, he has to play:

1 ...   K–K2

But then White plays:

> 2   K–B7   . . .

And now White controls the queening square and cannot be prevented from playing 3 P–Q8/Q, winning easily with a Queen ahead.

On the other hand, suppose that White moves first. You might think that's an advantage, but it isn't. This is what happens:

> 1   K–Q6   . . .

White has no choice, for any other move loses the Pawn.

But now Black's King has no move. The position is stalemate, and the game is drawn!

In Diagram 207, we have the same situation, a move or two back. Diagram 207 shows you how Diagram 206 was arrived at.

DIAGRAM 207

If it is Black's move, White wins. If it is White's move, the position is drawn

Note that the two Kings face each other. When they face each other on a line with an odd number of squares between them, we say that the King not on the move has *the opposition.*

As you will see from the following play, the opposition often decides the outcome of the game. If it is Black's turn to move, then the White King *has the opposition.* Result:

> 1   . . .   K–Q1
> 2   P–Q7   . . .

Now we have the position of Diagram 206, with Black to move. Therefore White wins.

But suppose it is White's move. In that case the White King has to move, and the *Black King* has the opposition and is therefore able to draw the game.

For example:

> 1   P–Q7ch   K–Q1

And, as we saw from the discussion of Diagram 206, White plays 2 K–Q6 and Black is stalemated.

Suppose White tries a different way:

1	K–Q5	K–Q2
2	K–K5	K–Q1!

Not 2 . . . K–K1?? when 3 K–K6 gives White the opposition (and resulting victory).

3	K–K6	K–K1!

Now Black keeps the opposition, and the game is a draw (4 P–Q7ch, K–Q1; 5 K–Q6—stalemate).

An important rule of thumb for these endgames is: when the two Kings face each other, with the weaker side's King on the first rank and the Pawn on the sixth rank, the ending is a win if the Pawn advances to the seventh rank *without checking*. The ending is a draw if the Pawn advances to the seventh rank with check.

The distinction is made clear in Diagram 208, where White's passed Pawn is further back. In such situations, where the passed Pawn has not reached the sixth rank and the stronger side's King is well advanced, the opposition plays a subordinate role.

DIAGRAM 208
White wins no matter who moves first

That is to say, the stronger side can either seize the opposition or *force* the weaker side to give up. In Diagram 208 we see what wide latitude the stronger side has if the passed Pawn is not yet advanced to the sixth rank.

If White starts first, he plays 1 P–Q6! seizing the opposition. If then 1 . . . K–Q1; 2 P–Q7 and White must queen his Pawn, as we have seen from earlier examples.

But what happens if Black moves first?

1	. . .	K–Q1

Now if 2 P–Q6?? Black draws by seizing the opposition with 2 . . . K–B1. Then if 3 P–Q7ch, K–Q1; 4 K–Q6 with the standard stalemate position.

2   K–Q6!   . . .

With this move White makes good use of the fact that his
Pawn is not yet on the sixth rank. Black's King must now give
way. For example, if 2 . . . K–B1; 3 K–K7 and White controls
the queening square.

2	. . .	K–K1
3	K–B7	K–K2
4	P–Q6ch	K–K1
5	P–Q7ch	. . .

White follows up with 6 P–Q8/Q and he has a quick mate
in the offing.

In all these endings White has a material advantage, which
makes it easy to understand how he achieves victory. But what is
interesting about the opposition is this: if we know how to use
it, we can win games where we have no advantage in material.
Diagram 209 shows such a position.

DIAGRAM 209

**If it is Black's move, White wins. If it
is White's move, the position is drawn**

If White moves, then he does not have the opposition, and the
game is a draw. For example, if 1 K–Q4, K–Q3; and White cannot
break through. If, however, it is Black's turn to move, his King
loses the opposition, allowing the White King to invade and capture one of Black's weak Pawns.

The essentials of the position in Diagram 209 are as follows.
With Black to move, his King must give way, allowing White
to capture a Black Pawn. Meanwhile, but a little too late, Black
will capture a White Pawn.

Then both sides will race to get a new Queen. White will
win the race, and later on the game, too.

1   . . .   K–Q3

Black's best chance. If 1 . . . K–B3; 2 K–Q5 and while White

goes after the Queen Knight Pawn, Black's King is driven
back, away from White's King Knight Pawn which he hopes
to capture.

2	K–B5	K–Q4
3	KxP	K–B5
4	K–B4	KxP

White is a move ahead in the queening race; the single tempo
is a slim but sufficient margin for victory, as we shall see.

5	P–N5	K–R6
6	P–N6	P–N5
7	P–N7	P–N6
8	P–N8/Q	P–N7

DIAGRAM 210

(*White to play*)
**White's winning process is certain but
lengthy**

Ordinarily, with a Queen against a mere Pawn, White would
have an easy win. Not so here, where the Pawn is already on
the point of queening and is supported by the Black King.

White's first task is to force the Black King *in front of the
Pawn.* The "why" will become clear later on.

9	Q–N8	K–R7
10	Q–R7ch	K–N6
11	Q–N6ch	K–B7
12	Q–B5ch	K–Q7
13	Q–N4ch	K–B7
14	Q–B4ch	K–Q7
15	Q–N3	K–B8
16	Q–B3ch	K–N8

Thus we have the desired position (Diagram 211) in which
Black's King has been forced in front of his Pawn. Black is
therefore unable to queen his Pawn, and this gives White time
to bring his King into action.

DIAGRAM 211
(*White to move*)
Now White has the win well in hand

White will repeat this process as often as he needs to, until the White King has approached near enough to figure in a checkmate. If it were not for this blocking technique, White would be unable to win despite his tremendous material advantage!

17	K–K3	K–R7
18	Q–B2	K–R8
10	Q–R4ch	K–N8

Again the Black King blocks the Pawn, and again the White King approaches.

20	K–Q3!	. . .

A finesse! After 20 K–Q2?? we have a stalemate position. (White also wins with 20 K–K2, K–B8; 21 Q–Q1 mate).

20	. . .	K–B8

Forced.

21 Q–B2 mate

Strange as it may seem, there are situations where the Pawn can force a draw against the Queen. Diagram 212 shows such a situation.

DIAGRAM 212
Black draws no matter whose turn it is to move

If it is Black's turn to move in the position of Diagram 212, the position is drawn at once, as Black is stalemated.

On the other hand, if it is White's turn to move, he has nothing better to withdraw his Queen and allow Black's King to crawl out of the corner. But once the Black King moves out, he is threatening to queen his Pawn. Then White has nothing better than to drive the Black King into the corner, when stalemate is again threatened. And so White can make no progress.

A Bishop Pawn likewise involves stalemate possibilities. For example, if you move the Black Pawn in Diagram 212 two squares to the right, White is still unable to win. If White plays QxP, Black's King is stalemated in the corner!

Diagram 213 shows an instance where a Rook Pawn is not good enough to win the game in an elementary King and Pawn ending.

DIAGRAM 213

Black draws no matter whose turn it is to move

The fact that the Rook Pawn is unable to win in such situations is an important bit of knowledge, and will sometimes enable you to draw what seems to be a lost position. Even the loss of the opposition does Black no harm.

Here is a plausible continuation from the position of Diagram 213, if White moves first:

1	P–R5	K–N1
2	K–N6	K–R1
3	P–R6	K–N1
4	P–R7ch	K–R1

Now White has only one move to avoid loss of his Pawn:

5	K–R6	...

Stalemate!

Going back to the position after Black's 1 ... K–N1, we can see why this position is a draw. If the Pawn was not on the Rook file, White's King could move diagonally one square to the right, with an easy win. But because the Rook file is at the edge of the board, White is unable to force the win.

On the other hand, in Diagram 214 the Rook Pawn is very

valuable. This is because it is a "remote passed Pawn." When this Pawn advances to the queening square, Black's King must scurry over to the Queen-side in an effort to capture the Pawn, However, as we shall see, the pursuit is futile.

DIAGRAM 214

(*White to move*)

Black cannot overtake the remote passed Pawn

Here is what happens in the position of Diagram 214:

1	P–R4	K–N2
2	P–R5	K–B2
3	P–R6	K–K2
4	P–R7	K–Q2

Too late!

| 5 | P–R8/Q | . . . |

And White, with a Queen ahead, wins easily.

In Diagram 215 we again see the power of a " remote passed Pawn." Once more material is even, which makes White's victory all the more striking.

DIAGRAM 215

(*White to move*)

This position shows the power of the remote passed Pawn

| 1 | P–R5 | K–Q2 |

Black, this time, is able to stop the remote passed Pawn—but only at the cost of renouncing his two Pawns on the King-side.

| 2 | K–B6 | K–B3 |

Black has no choice.

3	K–N6	K–N4
4	KxP	KxP
5	KxP	...

Now White's remaining Pawn queens without any trouble.
Black's King, far away from the scene of action, remains an
innocent bystander.

In Diagram 216 we see a winning manoeuvre which has many
practical applications.

DIAGRAM 216

(White to move)
**White queens first and this enables
him to force the win**

1	P R5	P–N5
2	P–R6	P–N6
3	P–R7	P–N7
4	P–R8/Q	P–N8/Q
5	Q–N8ch	K moves
6	QxQ and wins	

ENDINGS WITH MINOR PIECES

In Diagram 217 we have a fine example of a Bishop *v.* Knight
ending which greatly favours the Bishop.

DIAGRAM 217

(Black to move)
**The Bishop is definitely superior to
the Knight in this ending**

What are the factors in Black's favour?

His King is more aggressively placed—poised for invasion in fact. His Bishop is very powerful on the long diagonal, while the Knight plays a shabby defensive role.

White's Pawns are on *black* squares, and therefore they are permanent targets for the Bishop. The result is that White' set-up is strictly defensive, while Black has a powerful initiative To break through, he plays:

	1 ...	P–B6!
	2 PxP	...

Or 2 NxP, BxN; 3 PxB, K–B5; 4 K–Q2, K–N6; 5 K–Q3 KxP and the advance of Black's Queen Rook Pawn gives him an easy win.

2 ...	K–B5
3 K–Q2	K–N6
4 P–R4	KxP
5 K–B2	...

White's King must stay in the neighbourhood of Black' remote passed Pawn.

5 ...	K–N4
6 N–K3	B–K2!

The Bishop is headed for the Queen Bishop 4 square. Here i will guard the advanced passed Pawn which will eventuall reach Queen Rook 6. In addition, the Bishop will menace White' King-side Pawns.

7 N–Q1	B–B4!
8 K–N3	P–R5ch
9 K–N2	K–B5
10 K–R2	P–R6

DIAGRAM 218
(*White to move*)
Black has achieved his objectives

This is a perfect set-up for Black: White's King is tied down

by the passed Pawn. His Knight is tied down by the attack on
the King Bishop Pawn.

11	K–N1	K–N6
12	K–R1	K–B7
13	N–K3ch	BxN
14	PxB	KxP

White resigns, for the King and Pawn ending is easily won
for Black after 15 K–R2, K–Q6; 16 KxP, KxP, etc.

In Diagram 219, however, we have a situation where the Knight
is superior to the Bishop.

DIAGRAM 219
(*Black to move*)
Black starts off with a surprising move

White is handicapped by the weakness of his doubled and
isolated Queen Knight Pawns. These Pawns cannot be protected
by other White Pawns. They are therefore vulnerable to attack
by the Black Knight.

White's Bishop—and this is an important difference from the
situation in Diagram 217—has no targets. The Knight, which
has a distinct advantage, starts off with a decided surprise move.
Instead of playing the obvious ... NxP, Black plays to
capture White's Pawn at Queen Knight 5.

1	...	N–Q3!
2	B–N4	NxP
3	B–B8	P–N3
4	P–N4	N–Q3!

Now Black is going after White's remaining Queen Knight
Pawn. If White tries 5 BxN, then after 5 ... KxB we have a
King and Pawn ending in which Black plays ... K–B3 and ...
KxP with an easy win because of his extra Pawn.

| 5 | P–R4 | N–B1 |
| 6 | B–B5 | K–B3 |

Making sure of winning the Pawn.

7	K–K3	NxP
8	B–K7	N–Q2
9	P–R5	...

Black's defensive set-up is only temporary. Soon he will advance his passed Pawn and cripple White's defensive resources. As we study the situation in Diagram 220, we see that Black need only play ... P–B4 at a given point to free his Knight for co-operation in the job of advancing the passed Queen Knight Pawn.

DIAGRAM 220

(*Black to move*)

Black wins by advancing his passed Pawn

9	...	K–N4
10	K–Q3	K–R5

Now the passed Pawn, escorted by Black's King, is ready to advance.

11	K–B3	P–QN4!
12	P–B3	P–B4!

This frees Black's Knight from the irksome job of protecting the Bishop Pawn.

13	NPxP	PxBP
14	P–R6	N–N1
15	K–Q3	N–B3
16	B–N5	P–N5
17	B–Q2	N–Q1

White resigns, for his situation is absolutely without hope. After 18 K–B2, N–K3; 19 B–K3, K–R6 he cannot solve the double problem of defending his Queen Pawn and holding back the passed Pawn from advancing to the queening square.

When we turn to Diagram 221, we get a good idea of what the united Bishops can achieve.

DIAGRAM 221
(Black to move)
Black's Bishops are very powerful

When a player has two Bishops against a Bishop and Knight, he gains ground by cutting down the number of squares available to the Knight. As the comparative mobility of the Bishops becomes greater and greater, they come to monopolize the whole board.

1	...	B–B6!

Prevents N–Q2 or N–K1. This shows how the Bishops cut down the Knight's mobility.

2	B–B2	B–QB3
3	K–B1	P–B4
4	K–K2	K–B2
5	P–N3	K–B3
6	N–Q2	P–K4

Black's Pawns also share in the job of cutting down the Knight's mobility. For example, N–K4ch is impossible.

7	N–N1	B–N5
8	P–QR3	B–R4
9	P–B3	P–R4

Watch the advance of Black's King-side Pawns. By bringing the Pawns forward, Black hopes to turn the four Pawns to three into a clear passed Pawn.

10	B–Q1	P–N4
11	K–Q3	P–K5ch!

If now 12 PxP, BxPch wins a piece. Black now forces an ending in which he has an active Bishop against a passive Knight. In addition, his King-side majority of three Pawns to two can be turned into a clear passed Pawn. As for White, he has a Queen-side majority of three Pawns to two, but he cannot obtain a passed Pawn on that wing.

12	K–K3	PxP
13	BxP	BxB
14	KxB	K–K4

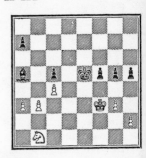

DIAGRAM 222
(*White to move*)
An unequal struggle between an active Bishop and a passive Knight

Black augments his advantage from move to move. His indicated course is to advance his King-side Pawns.

15	K–K3	P–N5!
16	K–Q3	P–B5!

If this Pawn is not captured, it advances another square to become a mighty protected passed Pawn.

| 17 | PxPch | KxP |

Now Black is ready to play . . . P–R5 and thus obtains a passed Pawn.

| 18 | N–Q2 | BxN |

This gives Black a won King and Pawn ending.

| 19 | KxB | P–R4!! |

Very important! Black prevents P–N4, which would assure White of a passed Pawn.

| 20 | K–B3 | P–KR5! |

The winning process that follows is very instructive.

21	K–Q2	P–R6!
22	K–K1	P–N6!

Forcing a passed Pawn.

23	PxPch	KxP
24	K–B1	P–R7
	Resigns	

Black must obtain a new Queen, leaving White helpless against overwhelming odds.

ENDINGS WITH A PIECE AHEAD

In endings where one player is a piece ahead he usually has an easy win. A passed Pawn, supported by its King and the extra piece, wins without any trouble. The position in Diagram 223 is a case in point:

DIAGRAM 223
(White to move)
White wins easily

1	B–Q5ch	K–N1
2	P–R7ch	K–B1
3	P–R8/Qch	...

And White's enormous material advantage will allow him to force a very quick checkmate.

The positions in Diagram 223 and Diagram 224 are almost identical. Yet Diagram 223 is a win for White, while Diagram 224 is a dead draw.

DIAGRAM 224
This position is a draw, no matter who moves first

In Diagram 223 the White Pawn is slated to queen on a square of the same colour as those travelled by his Bishop. That spells out a win for him.

In Diagram 224 the White Pawn is slated to queen on a square of the opposite colour to those travelled by his Bishop. That spells out a draw for him.

White's Bishop cannot command the queening square, which

is of the wrong colour. So White cannot queen his Pawn and he cannot enforce checkmate. As in Diagrams 212 and 213, he cannot win because of the peculiar helplessness of the Rook Pawn. Let's see some examples:

                1   P–R7   . . .

Stalemate! Suppose we try:

                1   B–K5

Again Black is stalemated.
Another try:

                1   K–R5   K–R2
                2   K–N5   K–R1
                3   K–N6   K–N1

And no matter how White plays, he can make no further progress.

In Diagram 225 we have a famous ending analysed by the great Philidor almost two centuries ago.

DIAGRAM 225
(White to move)
White has a forced win

This is one of the basic positions in endgame literature. In general, a Rook and Bishop (or a Rook and Knight) can win against a lone Rook in the most favourable positions. Diagram 225 is such a position.

Black's King, driven to the last rank, has his back to the wall. The White forces are ideally placed to force a quick checkmate.

White smothers the Black Rook's effectiveness with:

                1   B–B4!   . . .

Threatening 2 R–N8 mate. Black's Rook neither interpose nor check. So Black's King must do the best he can.

                1   . . .   K–B1
                2   B–K6ch   K–Q1
                3   R–N8ch   R–B1
                4   RxR mate

ENDINGS WITH THE EXCHANGE AHEAD

When you have a Rook for a Bishop (or Knight) you are said to be the Exchange ahead. When you have a Bishop (or Knight) for a Rook, you are said to be the Exchange down.

As the Rook is a stronger piece than the Bishop or Knight, winning the Exchange generally means victory for the player who has this material advantage. Diagram 226 is a good example.

DIAGRAM 226

(*Black to move*)

Black's advantage of the Exchange wins without much trouble

In endings such as this one, the Rook's superior mobility gives a winning advantage. But Black must know what it is all about, and he must marshal all his advantages. The first of these is to bring his King into a dominating position:

1	. . .	K–K2
2	B–N5	P–B4
3	K–K3	K–B3
4	P–QR4	K–K4

Now that Black has brought his King into an aggressive position, he can turn to his next assignment. This consists in converting his King-side majority of Pawns into a passed Pawn. The superior mobility of his Rook and the dominating position of his King are important contributions to achieving this purpose.

5	P–B3	P–QR4
6	B–B6	P–KN4!

Action begins on the King-side.

7	P–R3	P–R4
8	B–B3	P–N5
9	PxP	RPxP

Now, instead of three Pawns to two on the King-side, Black has two Pawns to one. In other words, he will soon have a clear passed Pawn.

10	B–K2	P–KB5ch!

DIAGRAM 227
(*White to move*)
Black will soon have a passed Pawn

White must now retreat his King, and either possible move
has its disadvantages. For example, if 11 K–Q2, P–B6!; 12 PxP,
P–N6!; 13 B–B1, K–B5!; 14 B–N2, and now comes the long-
awaited invasion with the Rook: 14 . . . R–KR1! Then, after
15 K–K2, R–R7; 16 K–B1, K–K6 Black has a stranglehold
on the position.

Now back to Diagram 227, and we will follow the consequences
of:

11	K–B2	K–B4
12	B–B1	R–K1!

A new phase: the Rook, which has only been looking on,
now enters the game actively.

13	B–K2	P–N6ch!

Note how Black keeps confining White's pieces more and more.
If White tries 14 K–K1, there follows 14 . . . P–B6!; 15 PxP,
P–N7; 16 K–B2, RxBch! This is an admirable illustration of the
power of the passed Pawn.

14	K–B1	R–K6

If White now plays 15 B–B3, he loses the Queen Pawn.
And if he tries 15 K–K1, Black wins with . . . P–B6! as in the
previous note. So, White tries a different way.

15	B–Q1	K–K4!

The simplest, although Black can also win by giving back the
Exchange: 15 . . . RxP!; 16 B–B2 (pinning), P–B5!; 17 K–K2,
P–B6ch!; 18 PxP, K–B5!, etc.

16	B–B2	P–B6!

Forcing a passed Pawn. Note how Black is always harping
on this victory-bringing theme.

17	PxP	RxBPch
18	K–N1	. . .

If White's King moves in the other direction, Black advances his passed Pawn and gets a new Queen.

18 ... R–B7

Resigns.

For after White's Bishop moves, there follows ... RxP, with further captures of the White Pawns to follow. This is a beautiful example of the power of superior mobility.

So great is the advantage of the Exchange that a Bishop or Knight, even when supported by an extra Pawn, should still lose against the Rook. A Bishop or Knight supported by two extra Pawns is a match for the Rook; victory will depend on the special characteristics of the position.

When the Bishop is backed up by three extra Pawns, as in Diagram 228, there ought not to be much doubt about the Bishop's triumph. However, as you will see, Black's win is not an easy win. The difficulty arises because White's Rook is very well placed for defensive purposes, preventing Black's King from penetrating.

DIAGRAM 228
(*Black to move*)
Black has a win, but it is a difficult one

Thus, if 1 ... K–B2; 2 R–K1! preventing Black's King from advancing via the King file.

If 1 ... K–R4; 2 R–KR1ch drives the King back. Finally, if 1 ... B–Q5; 2 R–Q1 and Black has achieved nothing. What makes Black's dilemna even more trying is that he has to guard his Queen Bishop Pawn with his Bishop. This cuts down the Bishop's mobility. After long study of the position, Black finds an ingenious plan:

1 ... P–N5!

Black sacrifices a Pawn in order to get another passed Pawn and to give his own pieces more mobility.

2 PxP P–B5!

The point. This new passed Pawn will eventually win the game for Black. White must do something about the threat of ... K–N4 followed by ... P–B6.

3	P–N5!	B–Q5!

Of course not 3 ... BxP??; 4 KxP followed by 5 KxP and White draws.

4	R–Q1	B–K6!

Very fine play. Black sacrifices a second Pawn; the reason why will soon become clear.

5	KxP	B–B8!

Threatening ... P–N8/Q. White must now choose between stopping this threat with his King or Rook. With one piece tied down to the Queen Knight Pawn, he is helpless against the protected advance of Black's other passed Pawn. This is the point of Black's Pawn sacrifices.

6	R–Q6ch	KxP
7	R–QN6	P–B6
8	K–Q3	...

White's King rushes to hold back the Bishop Pawn from queening. Black's King moves in to escort the Pawn to the queening square.

8	...	K–B5
9	R–N8	K–N6

DIAGRAM 229

(*White to move*)
Black's Pawns decide the issue

In this position White resigns. A likely finish would be: 10 R–N8ch, K–B7; 11 K–B2, K–K7; 12 R–K8ch, K–B8; 13 R–KB8, P–B7; 14 R–B7, K–K7; 15 R–K7ch, K–B6; 16 R–B7ch, B–B5! Now Black's Bishop Pawn can no longer be restrained from queening. An exciting, keenly fought ending calculated to a hair.

ROOK AND PAWN ENDINGS

As far as sheer statistics are concerned, there are more Rook and Pawn endings than any other kind. It is therefore useful to be thoroughly familiar with this type of endgame. The basic example, first analysed hundreds of years ago, appears in Diagram 230.

DIAGRAM 230

(*White to move*)

This is the basic Rook and Pawn ending

White's extra Pawn has already reached the seventh rank and is ready to queen—if only White's King will get out of the way. But the King is momentarily unable to move. The value of this ending is that it shows how White lifts the blockade and succeeds in queening his Pawn. Once he does this he will of course have an overwhelming material advantage.

White's first move—an important one—drives off the Black King.

1	R–QB1ch	K–N2

Now White can play his King out, threatening to queen his passed Pawn. But this would be premature, for example: 2 K–Q7, R–Q7ch; 3 K–K6, R–K7ch; 4 K–Q6, R–Q7ch; 5 K–K5, R–K7ch and the Rook keeps on checking until White's King again hides in front of the Pawn.

White therefore plays his Rook in such a way as to shield his Rook from the attack of the Black Rook.

2	R–B4!	R–B8
3	K–Q7	R–Q8ch
4	K–K6	R–K8ch

Black seems to be repeating the success in the note to his first move.

5	K–B6	R–KB8ch
6	K–K5	R–K8ch
7	R–K4!	. . .

Now the Black Rook has no more checks, and regardless of whether or not Black exchanges Rooks, the Pawn must queen. This position, or one similar to it, may well arise whenever a player is a Pawn ahead in a Rook and Pawn ending.

Another finesse in this type of ending is shown in Diagram 231.

DIAGRAM 231
(*White to move*)
White wins the ending by a finesse

Apparently the ending is drawn, for White cannot move his Rook without losing his Pawn. Meanwhile Black is ready to play . . . K–Q2 and . . . K–B2, forcing the win of the Pawn.

However, contrary to appearances, White *can* move his Rook after all.

1   R–KR8!   . . .

Note that 1 R–N8! would serve the same purpose.

1 . . .   RxP

Black has no choice, as White is threatening to queen the Pawn.

2   R–R7ch   . . .

The point! After Black's King moves out of check, White continues 3 RxR, with a Rook to the good.

Now let's see some Rook and Pawn endings which can be won despite the fact that neither player is ahead in material.

DIAGRAM 232
(*Black to move*)
Can Black win?

At first sight Black has an easy win because his passed, far
advanced Knight Pawn cannot be stopped from queening.

Our second impression is that White's command of the seventh
rank gives him a draw because of his standing mating threat.
If the Black King runs away from this mating threat he does not
seem to achieve anything concrete, for example: 1 ... K–N1;
2 R–R8ch, K–R2; 3 R–R7ch, K–R3; 4 R–R8 (threatens mate),
K–R4; 5 K–B5 (again threatening mate), K–R5; 6 K–B4 (still
threatening mate). And so the pursuit of Black's King goes
on—apparently endlessly.

Many a player with the Black pieces might give up hope of
winning; and yet the win is there!

| 1 ... | K–Q1! |
| 2 K–Q6 | ... |

Once more White threatens R–R8 mate.

| 2 ... | K–K1 |
| 3 K–K6 | ... |

Again White threatens R–R8 mate.

| 3 ... | K–B1 |
| 4 K–B6 | ... |

And still again White threatens R–R8 mate.

| 4 ... | K–N1 |

DIAGRAM 233
(*White to move*)
Black gains a precious tempo

By continuing to evade the checkmate Black has at last
managed to gain a tempo, for he attacks White's Rook, and the
reply 5 K–N6 would be meaningless. (Unlike White's previous
King moves, it involves no mate threat).

| 5 R–QN7 | ... |

The only move to hold back the Pawn from queening.

| 5 ... | R–R8 |

Threatening to queen the Pawn.

6 K–N6 ...

White is still threatening mate!

6 ... P–N8/Q

Resigns.

The new Queen stops the mate, and forces White to give up his Rook, leaving Black with an overwhelming material advantage.

In Diagram 234 White's winning problem is more prosaic.

DIAGRAM 234

(*White to move*)

How does White give his forces more mobility?

White's position is noticeably freer, yet at the moment he can make no headway. How can he get his pieces into action?

1 P–B5!! ...

This temporary sacrifice is the answer.

1 ... PxP
2 K–B4 ...

Now we can see what White gained by his Pawn sacrifice.

In the first place, his investment was only temporary, for he will immediately regain his Pawn. He has created a passed King Pawn—the Pawn that will bring him victory. This Pawn will be well supported by the activated White King, which will now penetrate into the heart of White's position.

Furthermore, new lines have been created for White's Rook. This piece can either occupy the open King Knight file or it can go to K3, supporting the advance of the passed Pawn.

The general effect of the temporary Pawn sacrifice, then, was that it turned White's position into one rich in dynamic aggressiveness.

2 ... R–K3
3 KxP ...

Black has no defence here.

Suppose, for example, that he guards his Rook with 3 ...

K–B2. Then comes 4 R–KN3 (threatening to obtain a won King and Pawn ending with R–N7ch!), and after 4 . . . R–K1 White plays 5 R–N6 (threatening R–KR6). Black has nothing better than 5 . . . R–KR1, but then 6 P–K6ch followed by K–K5 and K–Q6 leaves Black in a hopeless situation.

Black tries a different course, but his resistance is already flickering.

DIAGRAM 235

(*Black to move*)

White forcefully establishes a winning position

3 . . .   R–N3

Preventing White from invading via the King Knight file. But now the passed Pawn advances mercilessly.

4   P–K6   R–N5
5   K–K5   . . .

The White King is all powerful, while Black's King is degraded to passive defence.

If now 5 . . . K–B1; 6 K–Q6, K–K1; 7 R–KB3, R–N2 (not 7 . . . RxRP or 7 . . . RxQP, for then 8 P–K7 wins at once—such is the power of the far advanced passed Pawn!); 8 R–B5, R–R2; 9 R–N5 (threatens mate), R–R1; 10 R–N7. With complete control of the seventh rank White would have his opponent in a completely crippled state, forcing his resignation in a few moves.

5   . . .   R–K5ch
6   K–Q6   RxQP

It's too late for 6 . . . K–B1, for then 7 K–Q7 controls the queening square—a preliminary to 8 R–KB3ch driving Black's King away.

7   R–K3!   Resigns

Black is helpless against the passed Pawn. Thus, if 7 . . . R–K5; 8 RxR, PxR; 9 P–K7, K–B2; 10 K–Q7 followed by 11 P–K8/Qch. Or if 7 . . . K–B1; 8 P–K7ch, K–K1; 9 R–KB3 followed by R–KB8 mate.

A fine example of the power of a passed Pawn.

QUEEN AND PAWN ENDINGS

These endings require great patience and foresight because of the vast cruising range of the Queen. The advantage of a Pawn does not always bring victory because the hostile Queen may pick up a Pawn in return by means of a long-distance check; or else a perpetual check may snatch a well-earned draw out of what looks like a disaster.

DIAGRAM 236
(*White to move*)
White initiates a far-reaching plan

White decides on a bold and far-reaching plan: he will bring his King to the centre with a possible view to supporting his connected passed Pawns.

1	Q–Q3	P–B3
2	K–K2	Q–K3ch
3	K–Q2	Q–K4
4	P–QN4!	Q–R7

Black is desperate. He sees that if he continues with pure defence, White will carry out his plan. Black therefore seeks counterplay by capturing several Pawns on the King-side.

5	Q–K2	Q–B2
6	Q–Q3	Q–R7
7	P–N5!	. . .

White renounces the King-side Pawns; he realizes that the advance of his powerful passed Queen Knight Pawn is more important.

7	. . .	QxNPch
8	Q–K2	QxRP

If 8 . . . QxQch; 9 KxQ and Black's King cannot catch up with White's remote passed Pawn.

9	P–N6	. . .

The advance of this Pawn has become ominous.

DIAGRAM 237

(*Black to move*)

White has the kind of position he wanted

Black's Queen must dash back to stop the passed Pawn from queening. But 9 . . . Q–B1 will not do because of 10 Q–K7ch and 11 Q–QB7 driving off the Queen.

White is actually behind in material now, and his King will be unable to play the active role he hoped for. But it does not matter; the passed Pawn overrides any other consideration.

9	...	Q–Q2
10	Q–B4!	...

Threatens a pin with 11 Q–QB7, forcing a King and Pawn ending which White wins on the spot.

10	...	K–N3
11	Q–QB7	Q–K3
12	Q–B2ch!	P–B4
13	Q–N3!	...

Again offering a King and Pawn ending which would be dead lost for Black because of White's remote passed Pawn.

13	...	Q–K4
14	P–N7	Q–N1

Forced because of White's queening threat.

15	K–Q3	K–B3
16	Q–N6ch	K–K2
17	QxRP	Q–K4
18	Q–R7ch!	...

If 18 . . . K–Q1, White wins by 19 Q–R8ch!!, QxQ; 20 P–N8/ Qch. If 18 . . . K–B1; 19 P–N8/Qch!! wins.

18	...	K–K3
19	Q–N8ch	K–K2
20	P–N8/Q	Q–K6ch
21	K–B4	Q–B6ch
22	K–N5	Resigns

White's play in this fine ending was notably forceful and precise.
The play from the position of Diagram 238 is even more difficult
and requires even more ingenuity.

DIAGRAM 238

(*White to move*)

**Should White advance his passed
Pawn?**

Material is even. How should White proceed?

If he tries 1 QxP, QxP; 2 QxPch he can never hope to win.

But 1 P–Q6 (advancing the passed Pawn) looks very promising:
1 . . . Q–QN8ch; 2 K–B7, Q–QB8ch; 3 K–Q8, QxP; 4 K–K8
(not 4 P–Q7???, Q–N1 mate!). Strangely enough, in that case,
Black has a curious perpetual check by 4 . . . Q–QR5ch, etc.

1 Q–K6ch!   . . .

This move which creates a flight-square for the White King,
shows that White is well aware of the pitfall that has been set
for him.

1 . . .	K–N2
2 P–Q6	Q–QN8ch
3 K–B7	Q–QB8ch
4 K–Q8	QxP

Now it would still be a blunder to play 5 P–Q7??? because of
5 . . . Q–N1ch; 6 K–K7, Q–KB1 mate!

5 K–K8!   . . .

DIAGRAM 239

(*White to move*)

**White forces the queening of the
passed Pawn**

Black is fighting a losing battle. If 5 . . . Q-QR5ch; 6 P-Q7,
Q-N4; 7 Q-K7ch, K-N1; 8 Q-B7ch, K-R1; 9 K-B8 and Pawn
queens.

5	. . .	P-N4
6	P-Q7	Q-QR5
7	Q-K7ch!	K-N1

Or 7 . . . K-N3; 8 K-B8 winning.

8	Q-B7ch	K-R1
9	K-B8	Q-R1ch

If 9 . . . Q-N5ch; 10 Q-K7 and the Pawn queens.

10	Q-K8!	Resigns

For if 10 . . . Q-R6ch; 11 K-B7 dis ch and Black must resign.
The delicacy and precision of these last two endings gives us
a good idea of the qualities that are required to play Queen and
Pawn endgames—in fact, to play all endgames.